-Live Your Dash-

Discovering the 8 F's
to Freedom

By Jesse A. Cruz

Published by Pen It! Publications, LLC
812-371-4128 www.penitpublications.com

ISBN: 978-1-949609-13-4
Personal Growth / Inspirational
Non-Fiction / Self Help

Table of Contents

Dedication

For my daughter Faith, until we meet again on the other side of your dash.

January 6, 2017 – February 16, 2017 and beyond

Daddy loves you!

Introduction

Every day, we are witnesses of people choosing how to live their dash. We are living and breathing examples to others of how we choose to live ours. What do I mean by the term dash? The dash is the line you will have on your tombstone someday. The dates on your tombstone representing the time between the day you took your first breath and the day you take your last breath. That dash gives significance as to why those breaths matter. In other words, the dash is the legacy you leave to the world. The dash is a small inscription on the tombstone, but an enormous portion of your life. If you're reading this, your dash is still in progress. Each moment, your dash is telling a story to the world. What will your story look like from this day forward?

There are eight daily decisions of discovery which lead to freedom. These everyday choices influence the purpose and effectiveness of your dash. The layout of this book has eight chapters, and each chapter has multiple sections. By reading one section a day you will be able to reflect, learn, and apply the necessary changes to that particular part of your dash. Too often, people, try to speed through books and life, not knowing the meaning of what they just read or experienced. We all have different paces; however, taking the time to slow down is more impactful than trying to speed up. Life often feels like a race, but in reality, the brief moments we have been afforded, prepare us for a marathon.

Knowing that our choices directly impact the quality of our life, it would be wise to be thorough when making those choices. Following the dash formula, known as the Eight **F's,** will immediately improve your quality of life. The **F's** include **F**ocus, **F**riendship, **F**itness, **F**un, **F**inance, **F**orgiveness, **F**amily, and **F**aith. Each **F** will provide you with a guide to discovering your purpose. The way to reach your purpose is to make choices on purpose. The decision to develop your 8 **F's** will give you one of your greatest desires, **F**reedom. Anyone or anything that once held you back can now propel you forward. The same things that used to limit you will now set you free. One of the greatest benefits of living a dash filled life is the ability to choose how you will improve each area of your life. Choose to develop your **F's** and you will develop a legacy dash, one decision at a time.

FOCUS DASH -

Small Things

"Your life is always moving in the direction of your strongest thoughts."
Craig Groeschel

People generally tend to focus on the big things in life. This leads to underestimating the importance of the so called "small things." The small things are actually teachable moments we take for granted. What we believe to be an insignificant thing can actually become a monumental building block for our development. To further explain the importance of perceived small things, allow me to share this story about a family trip we took a few years ago.

My family enjoys hiking at state parks in New York. We heard of a beautiful place nearby and decided to visit for the day. We had big plans for this big park. We came for the BIG things, the big waterfalls, gorges and the big places to swim. We went on a hiking trip to Ithaca, New York, to a place called Robert Treman State Park. We saw breathtaking waterfalls like we have never seen before. We were mesmerized by their beauty. There were several trails, scenic views and even a swimming area that had a diving board right next to a waterfall. This was quite the experience in nature; one that we will never forget. During our hike, we decided to take a brief break to drink some water and cool off.

It was then that I picked up some small stones and began skipping rocks. Skipping rocks is something I commonly do to pass time when there is an opportunity. As I began skipping rocks my daughters looked at me with confusion and wonder. They didn't understand how a rock could appear to fly across the surface of the water without sinking. My children were intrigued and asked if I could teach them. I decided to demonstrate how I skipped the rocks several times. I showed them how I held the stone and the proper stones to use. They began trying and weren't able to skip them at first. Attempt after attempt they tried and tried. Suddenly, they were getting the hang of it. They began skipping the rocks. They were so proud of themselves; they had learned something new. After they skipped a few more, we journeyed back on the trails.

We made it to the swimming hole and made great memories. On the way back, we actually climbed up a waterfall, which, looking back now, was unsafe and actually stupid. It was dangerous, and my young children had no business climbing up this slippery waterfall. Don't judge me. Nobody got hurt, surprisingly, and it was a blast. It wasn't our best parenting decision, but it all worked out. It was a pure adrenaline rush. Once we finished the hike, we headed back to the car and completed our adventure.

On the way home, after hiking the unique trail, enjoying all the swimming holes, jumping off the diving board, climbing a waterfall, and seeing the unbelievable views, I asked my children, what their favorite activity was. They both said, "Skipping rocks, Dad". I actually became angry, confused and happy all at the same time. I was angry because we could have stayed home to skip rocks; I was confused because I didn't understand why skipping rocks were the best part of all we had done. Lastly, I was happy because they had enjoyed themselves. I thought to myself how could something so "small" be so impactful?

My wife and I came to the park for the big things; my children saw the big picture through the small things. You see, it isn't always the glamorous, flashy, and big things that make the impact we are seeking. For my children, it was skipping rocks that added value to their dash. Their dash became more meaningful because of their choice to experience joy through a small thing. At any moment, there is time to discover freedom in life, no matter how small the situation or activity appears.

You never know when your next experience-of-a-lifetime can happen. Now, when my children bring friends on hikes, they take the time to stop, and teach their friends how to skip rocks. Since the "small" idea of skipping rocks had a big influence on their dash, a rock on the ground is a teachable moment. It is during these moments of discovery, that we find freedom.

When we have freedom, we recognize that each breath we take is an opportunity to make a life changing decision. Knowing we will expire, gives us the reality that this exact moment should be cherished and appreciated. The date on our tombstone signifies the quantity of our life, but more importantly, the dash represents the purposeful quality of our life. The purpose of our dash happens one moment and one decision at a time, through the small things, even small things like skipping rocks.

Sight

There are millions of people in the world with glasses, contacts and surgeries to improve eye sight. Surgeries are designed to strengthen your eyes to have the ability to focus on things near and far. We spend more time correcting our sight, than we do fixing our vision. All the doctors and supports can help you see, but can't give you focused vision. We can look or gaze and even stare at something, and still be completely blind.

Have you been lacking in vision? Are you near sighted, only seeing the things directly in front of you? Or are you so far sighted that you miss what is right under your nose? Without proper vision for what is near, and what is yet to come, your ability to envision a prosperous life is limited. We first need brain and heart surgery before laser eye surgery. What's in your heart and mind determines how you see. What is inside of you will soon become reality on the outside of you. By being focused on focusing, you can change your prescription and see opportunities you never thought possible. Choosing to improve what's on the inside, limits your blind spots externally.

From Good to Great

You don't have to be a jack of all trades to feel adequate. Although, it's commendable to be well rounded and diverse, there are more efficient strategies to gain focus. Being well rounded is great, but well-rounded people are not world changers. A profound quote from the legend Bruce Lee states "I do not fear the man who practices 10,000 kicks one time, I fear the man who practices one kick 10,000 times". We often spend countless years trying to perfect numerous kicks, failing to realize it's that one special kick that is the best fit for discovering freedom. The dash isn't discovered by doing more things more times, it's revealed by doing one thing repeatedly. If there can be complete focus on one strength, you immediately improve other capacities of growth that are already in progress. If I become focused on the task of being on time, I become more dependable. When I am more dependable my wife and children will trust me more. My supervisor can count on me. Other family and friends all benefit from my one decision to focus on being punctual. Every decision has a domino effect on another area of life. Focus is not the ability to do well in several areas; it is the power of doing great in one, while impacting many.

Write It Out

I challenge you to write out the top 5 most important relationships and interests you have. For example, if my career goal is to be a fitness instructor and I surround myself with people who have no interest in fitness and live an unhealthy lifestyle, there might be a problem. The vision and relationships will be in tension and working against each other. It's time to build a dream team of dream chasers. Having a team of people who are also chasing their dreams, and reaching their own goals; leaves no time to get caught up in other people's nightmares. Team chemistry develops because the unit is extremely focused on success, instead of hating on you for reaching yours. If you are the lone wolf trying to form a pack to be like you, then you will be miserable. A team is always stronger when each person has different strengths. Individuals with a particular needed strength are helpful. If you went to the gym every day and only worked out your biceps how ridiculous would you look? You would have a ton of strength but would be extremely weak in other areas. Your bicep isn't the only muscle in your body; therefore, they all must be worked out together. Teams are like muscles that need to be utilized together to reach the desired outcome.

When you incorporate a group of people who share your vision and want to join you on the marathon dash, then you will be empowered, encouraged and supported in the pursuit of purpose. One set of eyes can only see so far and so much, while four eyes will always be better than two, especially if they are all heading in the same direction. To get to where you want to be you will have to see what you never saw. That happens by envisioning a hopeful future with others. When you change your lens, you change your life.

Busy

"Just let your 'Yes' mean 'Yes' and your 'No' mean 'No'"
Matthew 5:37

Your greatest strength in being ambitious can also be your biggest weakness if you neglect the comfort of just being still. If we develop focus fatigue, we will strive for the goal and lose ourselves in the process. The idea that if we are busy then that means we are busy doing the right things is a lie. Busy does not equal productive. There are millions of people who are busy at the wrong thing. Busywork is realistically a distraction from the purposeful investment of your time. When we say yes, to doing all these things to be helpful; we may be helping the wrong cause. Every time you say yes to something or someone, you say no to something or someone else. Try your best to not let your family be the ones you passively saying NO to by assertively saying YES to others. This doesn't mean don't give back and help, or never work, it means to be conscious of how you prioritize your time. Whenever you say yes to something or someone you are making the decision to say no to something and someone else. More work doesn't mean more results if the work you are doing isn't where your focus needs to be anymore. When opportunity knocks, go ahead and open the door. Just make sure you know when to close it in order to open up a bigger door. The opportunity you have is excellent, but it wasn't meant for you to stay in forever. Allow the vision to shift to something greater; don't become too comfortable with being comfortable.

Being busy is exciting and overwhelming at the same time. Choosing to be on the crazy cycle of being overcommitted, then complaining that we don't have any time is foolish. Being busy, even with powerful and inspiring things, can be your biggest downfall. Have you ever been there before? I have, and still struggle to juggle. A way to assess your priorities is to ask yourself, what your 5 most important life values are. Then based on your answers, write down what the 5 things are you spend the most time on. If your top 5 values and the top 5 things you invest your time in aren't the same, then we have diagnosed the problem. It isn't because of time that we lack the ability to do what's important; it is the mismanagement of the clock that has you snoozing through your alarm. Prioritizing time with the right people and the right causes, allow you to stop wasting your time on distractions life has tempted you with. When time is given properly, your life develops a solid foundation to build on. With a firm foundation you can build up to the next level of success.

Social Media

The present is truly a gift, if we learn how to stay in the present. Phones are very useful; but can be detrimental to focus. Unfortunately, it's impossible to be present in the moment while checking your phone. The phone literally takes you to a digital world, instead of an intimate real-life personal relationship with the human being right next to you. The closer you are to your phone the farther you are from your loved ones. Create a life where checking your phone is secondary. This is possible by being thankful for the priceless moment you are living in.

Interestingly, I was most distracted while writing this chapter. Focus over distraction needs to be at the center of any task. Distractions occur when you are unsure on how to prioritize your time. The reality of what exists on a screen is nothing compared to what lies in the hearts of your loved ones who are fighting for your attention. A crucial strategy for being social is to not use media as the primary method. Go ahead and have a conversation, look someone in the eye, laugh, smile, talk and then actually listen. One of our greatest resources is not our Wi-Fi connection, but in our human connection. Too often, when the Wi-Fi connection is stronger, the human connection is weaker.

Quiet Place

Find a quiet place where you can only hear silence; that is when ideas scream the loudest. Time in that quiet place can reveal your deepest desires and fears. This will take sacrifice; sometimes it's waking up a little earlier, or removing yourself from people for a period of time to think. The sacred time alone with yourself shifts your perspective and priorities. Get to know yourself. If you can't stand being alone in silence, chances are you are unhappy with yourself and need to work on loving you. Without knowing who you are individually in silence, you will never know the real you amongst the crowds and all the noise.

Heart Brain

One of the greatest places anyone can travel to, is the intersection of their heart and mind. That is where the toughest battle on earth exists. It's between those two elements where all wars are waged. Ask yourself the tough questions and give honest answers. What is the meaning to life? Am I focused on pursuing my purpose? What and who are the biggest distractions fighting against my destiny? How can I move one small step closer to being focused on what truly matters? Do I have peace? If this is my last day on earth what would be my one regret? Take a moment to ask these questions in silence all by your lonesome. Allow reflection to guide your direction. The more time you spend alone with yourself the more opportunities you will have to understand the focused dreams buried in your heart and mind. The more consistent quality of time you spend privately, the stronger you are equipped for victory publicly. To reach any victory you must know your opponent. At times that opponent is between the two organs keeping you alive. Seek wisdom for which to follow, brain or heart? When you are able to bring your heart and brain in unity, you will be able to make dash-focused decisions.

Quick Dash

In a moment's notice, life can feel like a flash and you have skipped scenes and are nearing the end of the film of your life. You have reached the end and you begin to reflect on what truly matters. I am a firm believer that it's not about counting the years we are alive but really living and counting those moments that give your life meaning. The dash may feel like a sprint when your focus is low, but when you slow down you can realize life is a marathon. It's not about how fast you run or how long you run, it's about why you run. Know your why and truly feel alive, one marathon step at a time.

Photo

Life becomes blurry when there is no focus. When we look at an out of focus picture, we have some clue as to what's going on in the photo, but we don't have a clear image. Some things are too dark or too light and distorted. When the picture is out of focus, we struggle to know what's happening in the photo. When things become blurry, we miss the small details that have profound impact. Blurry photos can come from moving too fast with the camera, and the same is true in our photo album of life. Moving too fast from one thing to another and never really appreciating the moment we exist in, leaves us unappreciative to the blessings we have. Allowing the proper time for the picture to develop will require a new decision from you. Everything included in your picture serves a purpose, and will direct you towards your vision or cause you to go blind. By removing timewasters that distract you, you remove the blur and fill your vision with clarity. If you don't get the picture, then go study some photos that have given your life, meaning, and purpose.

Just because your picture hasn't developed properly and is blurry, doesn't mean the camera is bad. It's a sign that there needs to be adjustments. Sometimes we throw away things and give up on them because the outcome was terrible when all we had to do was remain patient and make some changes. Focus, patience and preparation are essential, to having the picture in your mind become the reality you envision. On the other hand, too much exposure, or neglecting the right type of exposure can lead you towards a downfall. As you go into the darkroom where uncertainty lies, know that one focused step towards your vision will bring you to the light that you were meant to shine with. Go shine, despite the darkness for that is when your glow of purpose shines the brightest.

Become

What you focus on, is what you become. If you tell yourself every day, that you are going to be a great husband, wife, mother or father, most likely that is what you will become. When you think about something or someone your life direction shifts towards your thoughts. You will become ALL that you think you are, and what you don't think you are. You will become who you want to be and who you don't want to be, based on the thoughts you think. Thoughts are one of the strongest indicators of your reality. Choosing a healthy thought life leads to a focused reality. The power of your thoughts is monumental, influencing what you say, and how you behave. All wise or stupid decisions you have ever made, all started with a thought. Think about that! Any future decision that will add to your dash or subtract from your legacy will be based on the thoughts you think right now. Start thinking smarter and have smarter outcomes. Removing toxic thoughts, allows healthy thinking to take center stage in your life. Think your thoughts on purpose, and life will be purposeful.

AtTENtion

In this moment what has your attention? Maybe it's this book, or the sound of distractions surrounding you. Wherever your attention goes, you will follow. If I think about money I focus on money, if I think about health my focus shifts to health. If I think about drugs, then drugs have my attention. When something or someone has your attention, they essentially have a piece of you. Reflect on what and who has your attention most. That will reveal what and who is most important in your life. We give things our attention if we believe it's significant. By making a top ten list of what has most of your attention, will reveal what matters most. By taking those top ideas and ranking them all from one, being the least important, and ten being most important, you can physically see what has your attention. If the number one thing has most of your attention and is not the number one purpose of your life, then reevaluate and rearrange the direction of your energy and efforts.

You choose to create in your own mind what you should focus on daily. Even the word attention has the word TEN in it. Whatever you give your attention, should be a TEN, because whatever the thing or person is, has your time, which is extremely valuable. You are donating your atTENtion, and whenever you donate anything, it needs to be to a worthy cause or person. Focus on the Ten's in your life and stop stressing about the one's and two's.

Add Time to Your Day

Time is nonrefundable; make sure you are always content when you give something away that you can never get back. Even one hour, one minute, and one second can't return once it has been released. Time is leaving your expiration clock every second you are alive. If there were some way to give the precious moments more time, I'm sure you would take that opportunity, wouldn't you? If you could add a few focused moments to your day, you would make it happen. I know you would. So here is how that dream becomes reality.

Imagine for a moment if you could lengthen your day, imagine having a 36-hour day. What would you do with an additional 12 hours a day? The answer reveals something or someone you have been neglecting or a dream you haven't pursued. How about if you had 30 hours in your day, what would you do? How about just one additional hour a day, leaving you a 25-hour day. Now we can't add time to your day, but we can subtract some things.

Sacrificing some important things for extremely important things can get you closer to the twenty-five hours a day you long for. Twenty-five hours meaning more free time in your day to do what you choose to do. Focus one hour per day and you can become more productive throughout your day. Those precious 60 minutes are life changing. If you were able to manage your time more effectively for one hour a day you would have seven additional hours a week dedicated to leaving a legacy to your dash. It would give you approximately 30 hours a month to live your vision and 365 hours a year. This means more than 2 weeks a year to live your dash. What could you do with an additional 2 weeks a year? The answers are endless.

Those sixty-minutes per day, account for a lifetime of change. The sixty-minutes, doesn't have to be consecutive, it could be divided in blocks of twenty, fifteen or ten minutes. Either way if you can't schedule sixty minutes of time in your life to work on your life, then you don't really have a life to begin with. I know that is kind of harsh, and life can be harsh at times. Those sixty minutes, which turn into weeks per year, will improve your quality of life and your families for decades, all because of sixty-minute sacrifices of growth. There must be a time to regain focus to guide your decisions whether morning, afternoon, evening, or right before bed. Find a time at all costs and you will have priceless returns on your investment.

Mission

To start living, you will need to be driven by a mission. When you go to an agency or business, they will often-times have a mission statement posted in their building or on their website. If you were to write your own mission statement, what would it say? What are the highest priority goals for your life? Without a mission and focused vision, it's almost impossible to know where you are going. Secondly, it's confusing to understand where you are currently at and how you arrived at your present moment. Taking the time to write a mission statement is empowering and provides you with a hopeful future and purpose for being alive. The mission statement doesn't have to be paragraphs; it can be a sentence or a few. Either way, writing down the reason why you are alive will help you feel alive. Life won't be the heartbeat in your chest; it will be the reason for the heartbeat in your chest. What are you good at? Who is important to you? What makes you feel most alive? What brings joy to your life? Why are you here? What is your purpose? Answering these questions can guide you towards writing and following your specific life mission. Create your mission statement today!

Tongue

What follow your thoughts are your words; which will either build up or destroy others. Words are powerful and can give you confidence or bring insecurity and fear. You have the power to choose what you say to others and to yourself. What you say about yourself and others reflects what's in your heart. If you talk kindly about yourself.... you will do the same to others. If you talk poorly about yourself...... you will talk poorly about others. If we could see the impact of our hurtful words directly, we would have much less to say. If we could witness the healing power of our words towards others, we would all desire to become doctors. We could potentially heal one person at a time through one kind word, making the world a kind place.

Although, the tongue is one of smallest muscles in the body it holds the most power. Words can bring peace or war, change to greatness or wallowing in sameness, hope for a bright future or cause us to stay stuck in a dark past. Every day you chose the impact your words will have on your life and humanity. The tongue packs a more powerful punch than any fist ever could. Reflect on the conversations you have with yourself. Listen closely to the words you speak over your own life, for they will become a reality in the future. It's time to recognize there is a lesson in every word spoken and heard. What you chose to speak in word becomes rooted in action.

Thanks Again

Letting God and others know how thankful you are for them, changes your perspective from all of your problems.... to all of your blessings. Despite existing problems, giving thanks minimizes all of your problems and highlights your solutions. It's impossible to be miserable and complaining while giving thanks. If you are having an awful day, go thank someone. When you make a consistent choice to thank others for their efforts and who they are as people your entire being changes and the quality of life of everyone improves. Writing and talking about all the things you are thankful for will provide the shift from closed doors to open windows. When you give thanks, you release love into the world. Gratitude spreads joy to one person and dash at a time. We all release something into the world when we speak. Choose to release life changing gratitude changes everyone's attitude with one phrase, THANK YOU!

FOCUS DASH – PART II

"Focus on doing the right things instead of a bunch of things"

Mike Krieger

Anti-Social Media

I know this may come as a shocker to some of you, but your smart phone can actually make you dumb. You can have all the information in the world at your fingertips and still miss a priceless moment that can live in your heart forever. Give those thumbs a rest and face the test that's in front of you. Never being present and wishing you were somewhere else happens as soon as you take your eyes off real people and replace them with digital people. Too often, our gaze drifts from reality to reality TV, likes, and anti-social media. The concept of bringing people together through social media is convenient, and can be educational. Often times, it's abused and is an anti-social device. The phone can connect you to people all around the world, but won't teach you to love the person standing next to you.

In this technology era, the ability to multi-task has never been so easy, but how easy is it to carry on a conversation without being hypnotized by your phone? When we are too focused on our own desires, we can't help anyone else. It's all about I and our eyes. No wonder it's called an iPhone, or you can call it an EYEPhone because we simply can't take our EYE off it. iPhones, if abused, can steal our freedom. The technology prison removes us from our loved ones, and we become trapped and chained to a device. In prison, people are put in a place against their will because of choices that have been made. In technology prison, we buy the prison device and pay monthly on the phone to own us. Not only are we inmates, we are paying to be inmates. We become forced to check the phone by habit and fear of missing out. We can't work, sleep, or socialize without thinking about it. We have one eye on our children and spouse with another eye on Facebook. We have traded vision and focus with our eyes, to a screen that doesn't care if we exist. When you are a prisoner to something you don't get a day off. If you can't take a day off from your device guess what, you are a prisoner. You don't own the phone; the phone owns you!

Map It Out

When traveling from one destination to another a map of some sort is needed. Everyone has a map. The map is a guide to the goal. What is your map? Some people's map to success includes having money, fame, status and fitting in. There are countless maps we follow. We think we hold the key and we call the shots, but that's not true. There are countless factors that direct our steps that we have no control over. The key represents the number one priority in your life. The Key is essentially your God. The guiding light needs to be your focus, and knowing why you were created and who created you. Focus is key, but the key only unlocks the door when the potential is unlocked. What is the key to your map? What are you hoping the key unlocks to your door of opportunity that knocks? More importantly who is the locksmith to all of life's challenges? Whether you realize it or not you are giving your key of success to someone or something.

Grow

The legacy of greatness is reached when focus meets purpose through activating your strengths to improve society. In order to show your gifts, you need to grow your gifts. Growth happens through being watered with commitment not drowning in over commitment. By choosing the right amount of commitments you can grow with healthy pace instead of a hurried race. Once that has happened, then you can develop the gifts that you have been given. What you water grows, and what you starve goes. Take the time to plant what you want to grow in your garden of life, and remove the weeds that are attempting to stop you from the harvest.

Tomborrow

To add value to your tombstone dash you will need to subtract distractions. This is not the math you learned in grade school. You were told in order to add, you must increase. I believe to add you must subtract. Removing what is not part of your purpose will add peace to the piece you have been missing. In the dash equation, you will be called to subtract to get a higher number or higher place in your life. What is the one thing or person that can be subtracted from your life that you believe will elevate you to success? What or who is it that can be subtracted because of negativity? Go ahead name the person and thing that is holding you back. Some circumstances and people we cannot change, so we must change ourselves. Go and focus on what you can control and begin with simple math. Subtract bad and add good = Great.

A removal can be working less on work, and investing in marriage and family life, maybe it's less time with a friend or even some family members who are toxic. Think about the circumstances, friends or even family that could possibly be holding you back. Who and what makes you afraid? Fear was never meant to be a lifestyle; only a temporary reminder of what we need to change right now. Pursue the fear to conquer it. What you sometimes fear is the exact thing you need to pursue, because it's your worry that buries your potential.

Your Story

Take an inventory on the chapter of life you are currently in. You get to choose the character of your life story. In order for one chapter to end you must turn the page on what has been holding you back. If you are ready to turn the page to the next chapter, you will need to be willing to let go of the page you are on. When you let go of something and someone, you can now hold onto someone or something that will guide you in order to visualize your next step. You can't have one hand on the future while holding tightly to the past pages you were meant to let go of years ago. When you decide to let go of the small things that have tripped you up, your hands are now open and free. Your hands are free to receive huge blessings that have been waiting for you. Let go, so you can hold on.

ASK ASK ASK

"The man who asks a question is a fool for a minute, the man who does not ask is a fool for life"

Confucius

Having a trusted person you can ask advice from for decisions you are making, will bring you to a new level. Just ask! Provide them with an inventory of your life. Explain the purpose of your life or what they believe is your purpose, and witness if the purpose lines up with your actions. Above all, God is the one we need to ask before anyone else. God will not always tell us what we want to hear. HE will give us what we need to listen to. The less you ask the less you know; the more you ask the more you learn and grow. It isn't in the answers where you gain the most wisdom; it's the brilliance of asking the right question to drive you to the right source. Ask those who have the focus you aspire to have. The questions you are too uncomfortable or scared to ask are exactly what needs to be spoken to get you to the place you need to be. Never be too prideful to ask for directions, because it is in the asking that wisdom and answers are revealed.

What You Need?

Could it be the change you want, isn't the change you need?
Levi Lusko.

Think about what you want and need, and how the wants and needs should live in harmony. How you think, is reflected in how you communicate. Cluttered thinking translates into cluttered communication. Be specific about which thoughts you take captive and which you throw in the garbage. Everything you think isn't true.

Wanting a certain change does not equal the needed change. There is a difference. Needs trump wants in all circumstances. You could want something so desperately and pursue it your entire life, just to find out it wasn't meant for you or it was not what it was all cracked up to be. Wanting is one of the worst human characteristics we all have. Because of our wants we often neglect what we need. What do you need? What do you want? Many times, the answers are in opposition. It's much easier and comforting to do what we want, because doing what you need to do can be difficult. I assure you that doing what you need to do now, will allow you to do what you want later. Doing whatever you want to do for a long time limits your ability to do what you need to do when your time starts to run out. The opposite is never true. If you do what you want now you won't have what you need later. SOOOOOO stop talking about what you want to do and act on what you need to do.

It's not in getting more or having more, it's in becoming more. You actually become more by not having everything you want. If you had everything you wanted there would be nothing left to strive for in life; no purpose or reason to wake up and put in any effort because you have reached the pinnacle. The peak of the mountain is what keeps the climber going; knowing there is something more amazing and beautiful if you keep pursuing the goal, one step at a time. Needs are the water in your drought, and wants are additional rain after the storm. Sure, it's good to have enough rain, but having too much will cause you to drown. Having needs met first allows wants to be accomplished later.

UNcomfort

Focus is doing what's right instead of what's comfortable. If you become too comfortable, growth is stunted. It's the raging storm that brings strength, experience, and concentrated vision. The uncomfortable experience and people you encounter are not to be avoided, they are to be embraced. Avoidance of challenges will make life easy but won't help you improve the quality of life. Embracing the difficult waters of your soul allows you to grow beyond your circumstances. Anytime you are uncomfortable there is a chance for development. If you are comfortable every day, that means every day you aren't growing. Welcome discomfort, because discomfort is when we receive a wakeup call to being restored.

New Route

When the elevator is out of service, you need to know how to access the next floor. Focus is one step at a time, when the elevator is out of order. For greatness to exist, you will be exhausted and ready to give up. When you feel like giving up, that is when a breakthrough is around the next corner. Yes, the elevator is comforting; however, it doesn't teach patience in the process. Focus will guide you to a different path; which you previously failed to see; a path you never knew existed. However, the flight of steps helps you take flight to fight the battle of comfort and familiarity.

Download an App

The greatest experiences in life can't happen without pursuit. When you pursue something, you must take action. Knowing what your vision is, becomes useless if it's not applied. So many people take the time to download apps, because they serve a purpose for a specific want or need in their lives. Those apps are useless if they aren't applied. That's why they are called apps, apps meaning short for application. The greatest app in the world does nothing for you if there is no application. To use the app, it needs to be downloaded into your phone's memory, then opened with action. The more you apply the application the more useful the app becomes. The same is true when you have an idea or vision for something you desire to happen in life. With no application to your idea, you're just wasting the data of your brain. Learn, then apply, and then repeat.

In a Fog

Have you ever walked outside and noticed that it's foggy? I am sure you have and it's difficult to see what's in front of us. Driving in fog is even worse. Fog is dangerous because it limits our ability to see what's right in front of us. With our vision distorted, it's hazardous to move at the busy pace of life we are accustomed to. When focusing on one thing at a time our brains will not become clouded, but clear. We can prevent cloudy thinking and even cloudier decisions by not trying to juggle two ideas at once.

The concept of being an excellent multi-tasker only divides your attention and limits your ability to make healthy logical decisions. One thought and one action lead to one excellent decision. Next time you are having difficulty with making a life decision, stop what you are doing, and decide if your brain is in a fog or a cloud. Think about how many different directions your brain is taking you. This will require you to take a timeout in life and spend a few minutes in undistracted focused thinking about one particular thing or person. When you think clear, you will see clearer, and live crystal clear.

Seasoning

We all have unique preferences for the spice of life. Some need salt, while others want sugar. Knowing which specific taste you need, gives you options to feed the hunger of desire. There is always more than one pair of glasses to look through; and evaluate any given situation. Depending on the lens you look through; you could be limited to challenges or envision opportunity. What worked well for someone else could be a disaster if you had their same exact opportunity. The uniqueness of your situation is something only you can make beautiful. Someone else's life path isn't designed for you to live. Being different from the next person doesn't make you wrong, it makes you special. Because at this time in history there has never been, or never will be, a person that is exactly the same as you are.

Half Empty or Half Full

Take a glass of water, fill it halfway and really look at it. Go ahead…. actually, get up and fill it halfway, and observe the cup of water. People typically view the cup as half empty or half full. Two different perspectives leading to two different lives. The glass can represent real life situations (marriage, parenting, finances, career, education, etc.) Whichever glass you are looking at can be viewed as half full or half empty. We can focus on the water we don't have, which is the top half of the cup. Or appreciate the bottom half, which is extremely valuable. Instead of a half empty mentality (focused on what we lack), remain thankful for being able to have any water at all. Even a drop now is better than a drought later. Simply appreciate having a cup to put the water in to begin with. It's not that the water is half full or empty; it's that the cup is too big! Take the same water and pour it into a smaller cup. Now, do you have enough? By having a humble sized cup, (which is being content with less) your blessings become more. Behold, it's all about the perspective you have about the solution to your situation. The answer is not always more water; it's sometimes a smaller cup. Having the right cup is essential to have the need met. The smaller cup is having less wants, so you can appreciate the needs that have been freely given to you. As soon as you stop complaining, you can begin celebrating.

Every Day is Thanksgiving

Sure you have heard the saying let's not make mountains out of molehills. You need to turn your mountain of problems into a molehill of a hurdle. It is now a bump in the road instead of a dead end. Try flipping the telescope around on your problems. When zoomed in, something that looks so small and far away becomes enormous and overwhelming. When the perspective is switched, based on your thankful thinking; what used to be a magnified concern becomes so small and distant. Turing the telescope around is empowering because you can visualize a smaller challenge as an opportunity to boost your confidence to overcome the obstacle.

We Are Children

If our children stated they wanted to fix their problems the same way adults do, we would have a serious problem with that. A child who says, "I want to go to bed at midnight, not go to school, eat candy for breakfast, use bad language, disrespect adults, and not follow the rules," would cause adults to think this child is troubled and needs guidance. These ideas are not farfetched as most children feel this way from time to time. However, we would never let them do those things, even though that's what they want, but why? Because we know that doing what you want, although it can feel good, at times, is not right. Children have desires that are unreasonable and off the wall.

We don't allow it because we provide them with what they need, instead of what they want. Ironically, we struggle to do what we need ourselves, and expect our children to perform to a standard we don't consistently follow. As adults we are no different; we do things that we think "help" us because they are what we want to do. Yes, we want to smoke, drink, gamble, not go to work, not exercise, and eat junk food because it feels good. We do this even if it's destroying our future. All that stuff is easy, because it's a habit we have had for years. We are similar to the child who whines, and throws a fit every day because they have been allowed to for so long.

As adults, we whine differently. We become inpatient, restless, and impose our will on others. And instead of kicking, screaming, and crying in our room, we have adult-sized temper tantrums that destroy our health, finances and relationships. Stop throwing fits with gossip, laziness, comparing, and jealousy. Stop being an adult child. Do what you want, and you are childlike; do what you need, and you will succeed.

Choose Your Own Dash

We live in a world where we need to see in order to believe. However, we will believe the first gossip we hear without any proof. It's quite easy to fall into a trap with other people who are wandering down a dark path. We are adults trying to teach the next generation how to live, while being lost from out misguided choices. We often spend years aiming at a specific goal in our lives. We even hit the assumed bull's-eye and conquer the task in front of us, failing to realize we have aimed at the wrong target for years.

Seek out a mentor who has years of wise experience in target practice and inquire how they found their mark. Don't live someone else's dash. Yours is different from theirs. If you were supposed to live through someone else, or be like someone else, God would have made you into someone else. You are you, and nobody on earth can do what you can do.

There are specific gifts and skills only you possess. This doesn't mean you are a great artist and there are no other great artists in the world. I mean the specific style and message you bring to the canvas of the world is rare and almost extinct. There is only one of you. Nobody else on earth can do the things you are talented at, the exact same way you do them. It's refreshing to know that you are unique and special. The same way you are admiring others for their gifts, others are admiring you, for yours. One of the greatest gifts you can give to the world is to use the gift God gave you.

Focus Dash Goals

Identify 3 ideas, skills, or habits you will develop over the next 30 days.

1) _____

2) _____

3) _____

FITNESS DASH -

"Where the heart is willing it will find a thousand ways, where it is unwilling, it will find a thousand excuses"

Arlen Price

Fitness, is critical to overall health. Without being fit through exercise of the mind and body, our dash will surely suffer. The idea of purposely causing strain, with energy exerted and tons of sweat usually doesn't sound like a good time. In any discipline and great endeavor, there will be the temptation to not only skip, but avoid other productive commitments. One of the most challenging disciplines is to stay active. This doesn't mean hire a personal trainer and eat salad for breakfast. However, if you have any plans for living past today, taking care of your body is a good place to start. The body is what holds you together literally.

When you invest in your health, you invest in your future. The well-being of your mind and body is dependent on how you invest in your physical and mental health. Not all illnesses can be prevented. However, many can be avoided or reduced. By being intentional about living a healthy lifestyle your dash will be more impactful. The extension of your dash occurs with commitment to your health, which generates more opportunities for a purposeful legacy to be passed on.

BABY Steps

Becoming fit is not a huge step; it is more a series of consistent baby steps over the course of time. Similar to any meaningful success, small consistency brings huge gains and change. For some, a gym membership might be too expensive or inconvenient. If the gym doesn't work for you, try the baby step of walking, jogging, or exercising around your community. Each step is literally one step closer to health.

Please stop waiting for January to take your healthy seriously. You are better than that. There are too many excuses as to why fitness is not a priority. Maybe it's too cold, too hot, too rainy, and too nice out for a run. If you are waiting for the perfect weather and circumstance to get healthy, you will be waiting your entire life. Try working out at home. You only need your own body and space to exercise. There are apps, DVD's, and online workouts that will guide you towards healthy living. Technology allows you to bring the gym everywhere you go, via the phone in your pocket. It's quite simple, if you don't want to get fit you won't, and if you do want to, you will! There is no room to complain about something you willingly choose not to change. Now, make the choice to take just one step towards a healthy lifestyle, and one baby step into adulthood.

A Different Type of Fitness

The fitness dash isn't only exercising the body, but also the mind. Similar to your body, your brain needs a workout. Physical fitness is directly connected to exercising, but it's also true for the brain. For the brain to develop and grow stronger, mental exercises are critical to improvement in your mental state. We need to be challenged mentally to grow. Try reading a non-fiction book, watching a documentary, or learning a new skill. Without challenge to your brain, there is no strength in your mind. If you can't remember the last time you were challenged mentally, could it be that you are coasting in life? Coasting is comfortable, but will never take you where you desire to be. Coasting can't take anyone to the mountain top views we desire. New heights can only be reached by hitting the accelerator. Take some time and think about your thinking. Your thoughts have the power to build your dreams or tear them down. With all those racing thoughts you will need some time to let your mind rest. Exercise of the mind builds strength, and then allows you to rest during restlessness.

Feeling the Storm

One of the reasons people choose not to exercise their mind and body is because the storms of life have them struggling to breathe. Storms are challenges that happen to all of us. If each time a storm came along, we gave up; we would never reach our destination. We would be constantly wandering, with no idea on how to continue the journey. Storms range from unhealthy eating, sleeping and not exercising to serious health problems and a variety of other challenges. Too often the quiet storm of busyness creeps in leaving you with no time to take care of your mental or physical health. To know you are in a storm, you first have to identify a storm exists. Life is a series of heading into storms, or recovering from them. If any of your F's isn't what you hope they would be, a storm could be right around the corner. Be prepared, and adjust your sails to keep yourself afloat.

When the road is tough, keep persevering. Allow your fitness to let you finish. Too many people lose the desire for fitness because the unfairness of life has suffocated their hunger to achieve great health. For great results, you need great preparation. Get your rain coat, snow boots, and even your sunglasses out to prepare and protect yourself from the extreme storms may be in, as well as those approaching. Physical and mental challenges are the setbacks that set you back on track when you decide to be an overcomer.

Opportunities are disguised as difficulties. The hidden opportunities are steps towards building character that will help you to make it through the next storm. By choosing to get fit you will be able to enjoy the sunshine and endure the storms.

Motivate

I promise you by exercising your body and brain you will gain motivation for life. Balancing your physical and mental well-being keeps you in sync, ensuring that you won't sink. You will sleep better with an increased desire for a healthy diet. Embrace the freedom of being able to share your emotions, fears, hopes, and dreams, with others. When you do, your life will have a space that is filled with a renewed sense of inspiration. Every day you either make choices that enhance your fitness or destroy your fitness. Choose what is good for you rather than what feels good to you. Since we all have untapped potential, one of the best strategies to awaken our entire being is to consciously decide to live healthy. The potential within you is greater than the doubt within you. When you make the decision to choose health, a wealth of blessings will follow.

Daily commitment for healthy choices leads to healthy relationship outcomes. You will have a positive influence on your spouse, children, parents, friends, and your grandchildren by demonstrating discipline for your own well-being. The simple things such as reading and going for a walk consistently are enough to inspire your loved ones to join you. Yes, there will be days of soreness and exhaustion with packed schedules. However, without your health, you won't be alive to do anything or spend quality time with anyone. If you have goals to do anything in life in any area, chances are you will need your brain and body to reach the goal. Take care of your mind and *body* so you can be some*body*.

Decide to Thrive

Often, people believe they don't have time to work out. I proclaim you don't have time not to work out. Overall, if you don't work out, you will lose out. You lose out on more time, sleep, health and energy. By starting today, you will have the opportunity to gain many more days for your future. Even if you work out one day a week for 15 minutes, there will still be progress to be celebrated. By choosing to start, you are showing the world that you have decided to make a life change and your life matters.

You don't have to be a gym rat to exercise or even a house mouse to be engaged in the fitness world. You don't need a library of self-help books or a variety of specialized life skills. If you desire to live an extra 5 to 10 years, you can extend life expectancy by changing your expectations. Expecting a healthier, longer life, backed up with action will give you greater results. Don't beat yourself up for the current shape your brain and body are in. Take one step towards setting and acting on fitness goals. We all think life is too short and desire more time. That is why the dash on your tombstone is called a dash, because life flies by in a blink of an eye.

Fill-osophy

When participating in fitness, it's vital to have a fill-osophy. YES, FILL-osophy is what I said. The reason I say FILL is that having a motto, mantra, and vision will guide you to becoming fulfilled. What is your personal plan and FILL-osophy for fitness? Having a plan is common for most people. The follow-through of your plan is the difference between being average, good or amazing. If you want to be average have a plan; if you want to be good follow the plan temporarily, but if you want to be amazing then follow through on your plan as a lifestyle. No matter what you need to make a fitness plan. If you want to work out pick a gym, how many days a week and at what time you will work out. Write it down and commit to a healthier life.

The Body Mission

Your body goes wherever you go; you cannot escape or hide from yourself. Your body houses your organs which you need to live. Your brain and heart reside in the body. When was the last time you did some house cleaning? A clean house feels more like a home. When the heart and brain are not exercised, they are weakened, affecting your entire existence.

Without a healthy lifestyle the heart, brain, all organs and people around you are impacted. The body can shut down; preventing you from living the mission you have been given. We all have a mission. The mission can only exist with a healthy mind and body. The greatest mission in the world won't be completed if your mind and body are out of shape.

We are all called to a specific mission, but everyone has a common mission, to show love to one another. How we decide to reflect that love is the mystery. The mind and body are a gift and the gift. When the gift given is managed properly, it will change your life. Exercising the brain with the right thoughts leads to the right lifestyle. A healthy person has a healthy thought life; an unhealthy person has an unhealthy thought life. What you think is what you do, and what you do is who you become. Who are you becoming?

Sharp

The sharper your mind, the smarter your decisions will be. No different than a knife, your brain is powerful and can be dull or sharp. The brain becomes dull when it has been neglected. The key to having a sharp mind is by talking to people who are smarter than you. Trust me, they do exist. Even a fool can school you if you have too much pride. Nobody is ever too successful, rich, or important to seek out wise council from others. You are ignorant to many things in life, no matter how smart you think you are. All great successes came with assistance. It takes teachers, coaches, parents, siblings, neighbors, family, friends, mentors, counselors and countless other people to be an ingredient to the recipe of fitness. To be great we need to want it more than anyone else. Working on you is a full-time job and you do need some overtime. The overtime pay is excellent because it provides significance, character, perseverance, and dedication. There is no instant success. When you want to improve, it will take time, commitment, and training. Only when you excuse your excuses will you reach the summit of victory.

The people in your life are strategically placed there to teach you specific life lessons. The individuals you find most annoying and incompetent, will probably teach you the most. They will reveal things about you that you never knew existed. Every human being you interact with has something to teach you, if you remain teachable. By being in constant student mode, you can break the mold of stagnant thinking and breakthrough with ground breaking ideas. Acknowledging you don't know it all, brings you one step closer to knowing more. To grow more, you first have to acknowledge you need to know more.

You will have to be hungry with a desire to learn and apply the knowledge you have gained. New knowledge is new life. The more wisdom you seek, the faster you will find yourself. Allow the people in your life to sharpen you, so you can cut through the barriers that have been holding you back. Let the experts empower you in areas, where you are still learning. Life is a team effort and you need to rely on others to help you in specific ways. Even the greatest minds in history had some assistance along the way.

beneFITS

We all have either struggled with depression or know someone who has. One of the greatest ways to combat concerns is to rebuild connections through rebuilding relationships. When you recognize and begin using the God-given talent you have been given your life completely changes. Activating your gifts helps you to have a positive self-identity. Having a healthy relationship with yourself, is paramount to having it with others.

Think of your favorite athlete, musician, actor or someone you truly admire for the skills they have. Why do you admire them so much? You admire them because their pursuit of their dash has inspired you to discover the purpose of yours. Our heroes have a specific gift that they are sharing with the world. They constantly remain fit in mind and body. They constantly train to grow, improve, and strengthen their dash. We applaud their accomplishments, accolades and awards. It's easy to overlook the time, effort, energy, and commitment it took for them to become world class athletes, musician's doctors, actors and so on. Their rise to the pinnacle of their profession had nothing to do with being lucky. It is rather commitment, applied with a disciplined lifestyle. They all decided to go after the benefits of success; but first they needed to FIT with their gifts. There are always more behind the scene struggles than there are big screen successes. You too also have a gift, now it's your turn to let your light shine for the world to see. We are always in the editing process, however, if you remain patient your breakthrough is approaching.

One of the biggest differences between good and great is that good became discouraged during challenges, while the great expect, and accept the obstacles in their path. Without the challenging circumstances, our role models wouldn't even exist. We become trapped by comparing our failures to other's successes. It's not the successes that make anyone great, it's the temporary failures that do. When failure tries to tell you to quit and you keep going anyway, that's how you become successful. When you first feel the pain and keep going, that is when your greatest growth occurs. When you feel like you have nothing left, give just a little more. Just do one more rep, read one more page, do one more thing that will prepare you for victory. All successful people were once temporary failures who refused to quit. Remember, to be fit is to refuse to quit.

FITNESS DASH - PART II

"Your body can stand almost anything. It's your mind that you have to convince"

Unknown

Tough Decision

Even without making a specific decision, a decision has still been made. Without moving forward in fitness, you move backwards in health. Think back to those heroes you admire, you can be a hero for your spouse, children, friends, and community the same way those heroes have impacted you. On the days when you grow tired, and don't want to pick up those weights or open that book, think of your dash Write one sentence that will represent the legacy you desire to leave to the world. The decision to be fit is a decision of wisdom. Wisdom often comes with the sacrifice of short-term comfort for long term peace. If you aren't making any uncomfortable decisions, you're not growing. You're only going back to the person you used to be. Who wants that? The way to be tough is to make tougher decisions.

Gym

Perhaps, the word gym is intimidating or being fit is simply too much work. Possibly the term *health club* sounds more approachable or maybe even *extended life exercises*. Whatever name you call it, don't wait another day; your life depends on the decision to start and continue down a healthy path. Inspire an entire generation by your ability to generate new energy towards the path of healthy living. Give those thumbs a rest from scrolling and get rolling on an exercise that will truly give you the results you hope for. The gym is your friend, refusing to go, is your enemy. It's time to go hang with your long-lost friend.

How You Feel?

Have you ever worked out and later your muscles hurt? You probably have! That is because your muscles are breaking down, so they can rebuild themselves. A breakdown in muscle is the first step towards rebuilding and repairing. Quitting because of pain would ruin potential gain, not only in your muscles, but in your character. Deciding to not workout because of the pain, only leads to more pain. Ironically, we think by avoiding the exercise, we avoid the pain and are safer. Just the opposite is true. This is similar to the person who complains about losing weight but makes no effort to be fit. It simply doesn't add up!

The pain you are experiencing wasn't designed to leave you permanently hurt. There really isn't long term healing gains, without short term painful gain. Without the pain of struggle and discomfort temporarily, your entire body will suffer over the long haul. The pain will either stop you or motivate you. Do you really want to quit at every obstacle, or do you want to find a way to conquer the task that's in front of you?

Most people want growth, but don't want to endure the pain required for growth to occur. Weaknesses are indicators on how we can become strong. We go from lacking many things, to lacking nothing by having the right mentality. The temporary weakness you're feeling is preparing you to go beyond a place you ever imagined. When it's your time to heal in those moments of weakness, you will need to stretch beyond your limitations and push to the next level of a fit mind and body. The pain was never meant to stop you, but to propel you toward your calling.

Everyone gets knocked down and that's okay. What's not okay is to get knocked down and stay there. Nothing can be truly fixed, without first accepting something is weak or broken. There aren't limits to your greatness, only the limitations you place on yourself, and the people you give permission to discourage you from success.

The pain of change is always less painful than the pain of staying the same. As the soreness occurs, there is the option to let the pain break you or make you into the person you aspire to become. The temporary hurt will improve you as a parent, spouse, family member, friend, employee and person. The heavy lifting and carrying of baggage can't be carried without resilience. We all can heal more efficiently if we allow others to help us carry our hurts.

Fit Mind

There are times to exercise the body and mind, but also times to rest. It's weird to think that rest is a form of being fit. Some people might think relaxation and rest are for the lazy. Actually, the body and mind are designed to need rest and without it, you damage your life for the long term. Just rest, breathe and relax. Certain times in life it is more beneficial to remain still, than head into motion. When you are stressed, anxious, and emotional, these are cues that your mind and body need relief. Relief in the form of rest will give the belief you are the best, the best at being fit for the fight. Sometimes the greatest thing you can do for you, is rest.

Goal For It

Setting goals are guides to our desired direction. Action plans for achieving goals well keep your brain in shape. If a person writes down their goals, they are more likely to complete the goal. If I set a goal to lose 15 pounds in one day, this is a great goal, but unrealistic. While writing it down increases the chances it will happen doesn't mean it will happen immediately. Results require commitment to effort, the greater the effort, the greater the reward. Aim high when writing your goals, so if you do not fully reach them, you will still have achieved another step towards greatness. Writing down your goals, forces your brain to visualize them motivating you to turn them into reality. Put your goals in a place where you can see them throughout the day. Tape them to the fridge, bathroom mirror, bedroom door, car dash board, at work, any place you breathe air. I promise it will positively impact your quality of life. Use those sticky notes until the goals stick with you everywhere you go. Soon, everywhere you go another goal will be achieved.

Goals can be achieved alone, but can come to fruition much faster when they are shared. Before we can lead others to the fit life, first we must be led. When you are determined and have surrounded yourself with other fit-minded, determined people, you will be inspired to persevere when you feel like giving up. Sharing your goals with family and close friends holds you accountable. Goal sharing not only benefits you; it benefits the people you share it with. Your commitment to change inspires others to reflect on their own need for change. Your goals need to become so great that they are impossible to achieve alone.

A Moment

Nobody in human history became great because of great excuses. High complaint levels indicate low commitment. If you don't have time to do a push up, go for a walk, or do something to benefit your health, then you don't care enough about your body. Not making the time to pick up a book or ask a question to someone who might know something more than you, is foolish and sets you up to fail. It only takes a moment to invest in your mind and body, but a moment not invested can be a lifetime wasted. As each moment passes, so does the option to gain some health or some hurts. Scheduling brief dedicated moments of improvement builds your foundation for a lifetime. One moment is all it takes to rust or restore your body.

Can't Go Far Without a Car

Imagine your body is a car and it needs fuel to go from one place to another. When a car needs an oil change, break job, new tires, or other maintenance, people typically provide the car with what it needs. Some may fix it themselves or go to a mechanic shop. We can often see the importance of the upkeep of a car to make sure it's running smoothly. We often fail to realize the life or death implications of fitness. The car symbolically represents the body we exist in every day. The body, like the car, needs regular maintenance. The car needs gas, oil, and other fluids that cause or help the car to run properly.

Similarly, the body needs food, water, sleep, and exercise of the mind and body to run properly. Sure, you can skip regular maintenance for your body, but you will become sluggish, running on fumes leading to bigger mechanical problems in your organs. The same is true of your mental health. You might blow the engine; how far will you go in life on a blown engine? The blown engine comes from lack of self-control, patience, and a variety of other mechanical and interpersonal challenges. You might be in need of a new transmission because addiction, abuse, and neglect have haunted you your entire life. The symptoms of not taking care of yourself could lead to a flat tire of stress, depression and anxiety. Maybe your car tires are about to blow while you're driving, causing a reckless destruction of mental illness. The maintenance of your car is important, but not in comparison to maintenance of your health.

All of this can be prevented by regular maintenance on your body. Do you currently have a maintenance plan? Is your oil being changed when needed or are you overdue? Oil changes in our body need to happen daily. Refueling keeps the car not only running, but thriving. What good is it for a car to start and be unable to drive? This is like waking up out of bed in the morning and not being able to move into action? It's not enough to wake up from sleeping, everyone does that. The gym, sleep, books, diet, education are the mechanics you need daily to fix your dash before it becomes too broken to fix. We have the tools, but tools are no good if we don't use them properly or educate ourselves to know we even have them. Let your fitness be a witness to greatness. Too much time is being spent on replaceable things, and not enough on our irreplaceable lives. Ask yourself, what's more important, maintenance on your car or on your body?

Love Yourself

How you feed yourself is a direct demonstration on how you love yourself. When you understand that you are lovable and important you begin to feed your mind and body with the proper nutrients. If you think low of yourself will put garbage into your mind and body. When you look at yourself as treasure instead of trash, you will value the riches of your entire being. We often neglect what we don't believe to be important. If you have neglected yourself, it's because you have labeled yourself as insignificant. Try to relabel yourself. You are awesome, amazing, and valuable. You can beat the odds and you are greater than how you see yourself. When you start to love yourself, you will treat your mind and body with the exercise they deserve.

Heart Attack

"The pain you are feeling now is nothing compared to the joy that awaits you."

Romans 8:18 (NIV)

Not making the effort in fitness causes more heartache for your life. Those who do not engage in physical activities are more likely severe health problems. Your mind also brings mental health challenges. Your body and mind are essentially under attack from your own mind and body. When your mind and heart are neglected, they act out. They act out in ways of sickness and mental health. Similar to how children act out when their needs don't get met, so does our brain and heart. However, there is a remedy. It's called LEARNING and EXERCISE!

Business

Thinking is serious business. Being intentional about recognizing patterns in your thought life can reduce the impact of negative thinking. Once you label the negative thoughts you will have much more control of your actions because you can connect how your thoughts and actions are directly linked. Some people have negative thoughts in the morning and for others it's at night. For most of us, especially me, awful thoughts happen when I am hungry, so watch out! For others, it's during holidays or when it's cold or raining. It can be in social situations or other triggering events. Knowing what thoughts you are having, and why you are having them strengthens your ability to have a fit mental health.

You have the freedom to choose to go from being limited, to being challenged. The thoughts you allow to take root, will take you on a different route. Acknowledge the thought, determine if it aligns with your overall fitness dash and adjust from there. Think on purpose about what is best for you at the end of your life, so the end of your life doesn't happen sooner because of toxic thinking.

Now What?

Why do we choose short term success over long term significance? I believe its delayed gratification. We want what we want, and we want it now. That's a trap we fall into. Instead of knowing there will be a delay to our success, let's have it all now! This causes more long-term problems than any short-term solution. We desire going to the gym one time and achieving the overnight weight loss. We enjoy fairytales because of the happy ending. People forget about all the struggles and battles that led up to the happy ending. It's time to wake up and shape up. Patience can often be the biggest hurdle toward reaching any goal. If you learn to actively wait, you can reach your ideal weight.

In a world of Google, Siri and smart phones, perhaps we've become more inpatient. We are one click away from the results we want. This method is convenient, but it spoils the hard work and deceives us into thinking we can take short cuts on everything. That is the deception of the one click trick. With one click we can have all the answers to life. We should work harder on ourselves than anything else. Our phone can be a useful tool, but one of the greatest hindrances to our success. We would rather bury our eyes, and compare our lives, to someone else on social media, than focus on our own health. We want to lose weight and get smart as fast as Google tells us how to. Patience is a dying virtue, if you possess patience you will be one step ahead of the old you. It is during the waiting, when true character erupts towards an explosion of greatness or a meltdown of failure.

Resume

Knowing the truth without application is like having a burned-up resume. If someone asked you for a personal resume on how you are taking care of yourself with physical and mental health, what would your resume say? How long would your resume be? I am sure your work experiences are loaded with all kinds of stuff. Does your physical and mental health resume mention the stress, workaholic tendencies, and laziness? The longer your fitness resume, the more aware you become of the gifts you have. Your challenge is to create and highlight your personal fitness resume with what you are doing, and where you can grow. Your resume for life needs to match the purpose of your dash. Build your resume on significance through your health. Your life will only go as far as your health will take you. If you take your health seriously then your fitness will take you past your past leading to a powerful future.

Fitness Dash Goals

Identify 3 physical/mental exercises and how frequently you will engage in each activity over the next 30 days.

1)_____

2)_____

3)_____

FRIENDSHIP DASH -

"Your friends determine the direction and quality of your life."
Andy Stanley

There are many people we call friend, but very few are identified as a friendship. Ask yourself, "How many friends do I have?" Go ahead; name them. What is your number? Five? Eight? Ten? Or if you think you are really cool, maybe twenty? If I were to ask you how many of those relationships/ friendships are mutual I believe the number would decrease quite dramatically. The number most likely would be less than five if you decipher the difference between friends and friendship.

The question is what is friendship? We all have our own concept of what makes a friendship, a friendship. Friend can be a more generalized term, while friendship is a strong bonded relationship. Friend*ship* and relation*ship* are words that both have the word ship at the end. Ship is at the end of the word because to work properly they need to be steered in the same direction. When both are working together, they achieve more than they ever would have separately. To reach your destiny you will have to assess your circle of influence and which direction you want your circle to travel. Any desired outcome will take a team to get there. When times become tough, the strength of friendship provides oxygen to a place where you were once suffocating. Friends will abandon ship, while friendships will jump in and save you when you have fallen over board.

Quick Assessment

By taking this friendship assessment below, you will become more aware of how to intentionally choose healthier friendships. Take a moment to visualize what true friendship looks like in your life, or what you hope it would look like. Fill in the name of the people you think would fit into these blanks with a pen or pencil. Some of this content below is from a conversation I had years ago with an individual that truly helped me evaluate what true friendship looks like.

Would you let _____ have a key to your house and not worry about anything? Would you let _____ watch your children? Could _____ be around your spouse for a moment, and you would have no worries about anything questionable happening? If there was a group of family members, teammates, friends, students, coworkers, church members, all gossiping about you, do you believe _____ would stand up for you? Would you let _____ drive your car? Could you loan _____ money and know without a doubt they would pay you back without having to harass them? If you had a crisis would _____ stop what they were doing if they could, and come, see you and support you during your difficult time? If you were in the hospital, jail, rehab, or moved far away, would _____ come visit you? For the friends who live far away, does _____ call, or text to stay in contact?

Would _____ let you live in their house if some disaster happened that wouldn't allow you and your family to live at home anymore? If you became sober, quit drinking, smoking and doing drugs would _____ still be around? If you were in prison for several years would they write, take phone calls and help take care of your family? If you had a serious health condition would _____ help take care of you and your family? If you didn't have money or status with no job, car, power or material possessions would _____ still have your back? If you opened up a business, would _____ come support, it and tell others about it? If you fell into addiction, or had a dark secret could you share it with_____? Who can you completely be yourself around without ever feeling judged _____? Who loves, trusts, respects and has your best interest _____?

These questions might be difficult to answer. Chances are, if you are struggling to fill in the blanks, you might not have people who have given you their friendship, or you haven't given others your friendship. Most likely it's a combination of both. It's not too late to start new friendships. If your circle is not what it should be, begin a new one. Some relationships happen because of circumstance because of work location and your community. However, you still get to choose who you let influence your future.

Use this assessment as a guide, not the deciding factor for the rest of your life. Witness what name appears most and the ones who barely appear, or are nonexistent. Decide who needs to be removed, who needs to stay and who can be added. It's not too late to make an adjustment to the strength of your circle by removing the weak links. Your dash will be strengthened by becoming aware of the answers in the assessment. Acting on these results will bring your dash meaning for the rest of your life.

Learning more about the friendships you have or don't have isn't designed to depress or discourage you, it's meant to bring awareness to how your current choices in friends have influenced your current situation in life. The design is to create a vision of what type of friendship you want and need in life. More importantly after answering all those questions are YOU giving the right type of friendship to others? Could you put your own name in all of the blank spaces to assess how you treat your close friends? Answer all of them honestly. This is not designed for you to think "Oh boy, I have no friends, and I don't know how to be a good friend either". This is a wake-up call.

Friendships have more of an impact in your life than you realize. We all desire to have a stronger circle of peers, but you first need to become the strong individual in your own personal life. We attract what we want in life. When you become what you desire, you attract others who desire the same thing. If you want a sports fanatic drinking buddy, I can guarantee you will find one. If you desire surface level friends who have no depth, they are easy to find. If you desire a friendship that will inspire you to grow and develop your character and inspire you, you will find that as well. You will attract the kind of friend that you are to other people. Attraction is powerful, what you attract will either knock you flat on your back or be a spring board to help you bounce back.

Chosen Family

Friends come and go, but friendships are special. Friendships become family members. Sometimes our friends are closer to us than our own family. A huge benefit to the friendship relationship is you can always choose who will fit into those blanks. Some friends aren't a good fit, while other's compliment you perfectly. Some chosen family members we have known our entire lives, and some have crossed our paths recently. It is not in the length of the relationship we have with others; it is in the depth of the bond that matters.

Sometimes, the best friend you have had since middle school or high school provides you with security from your childhood. All the childhood memories shared together provide a feeling of comfort. Unfortunately, we tend to hold onto friendships longer than we should because of past history. There is such a thing as maturing out of friendships. Sometimes our childhood friends take a different path in life. The path they are on does not match or line up with our values, beliefs or morals.

I am not saying cut them off because they think differently. If a friend is looking to get sober, then hanging with your friend who is still using drugs is foolish. How about the family man hanging with his friend who is single with no children? On the surface there is nothing wrong with that at all. But if the single guy is trying to get the family man to party hardcore and neglect his family, this would be disastrous. You might have to reconsider the friendship, not because you don't love them or aren't loyal, but you are more loyal to your future and your family's success.

The friendship dash can be damaged when we bring those who should have been left in our past, and were brought right into our future. An effective friendship dash will require the sacrifice of some relationships. Not all relationships are meant to be in the current season of life you are experiencing. Past friendships should be the downgraded version of current friendships. Your current friendships should be the downgraded version of future friendships. If you can't see any improvement between past friends and current friendships, then you need to adjust your friendships standards.

Too Much

Prioritizing to spend time developing friendships is a bond that should never be taken for granted. Life does get busy, and we can lose sight of important relationships. Chances are if you don't have the time on a regular basis to make a phone call, send a text, e-mail, or make time to meet if you live close by, most likely, you have too much going on to be a friend at all. With all the things of this world fighting for your attention, don't let distractions make a subtraction, from the friendship equation. I know being busy helps you feel good about yourself, but friendships are more important. If you do become distracted, don't allow it to be from spending quality time with quality people helping you develop a quality life.

Knowing which things are most important is crucial to having a healthy balance in life. People have their own idea of what and who comes first. When things aren't put in proper order in our relationships chaos is sure to follow. We all have several roles from being a spouse, parent, family member employee, etc. Even having those important roles shouldn't prevent you from forming and keeping friendships. The other relationships you are committed to should motivate you to be an even better friend than ever before. By modeling dedicated friendships for your spouse and children they will learn the value of having their own healthy friendships. When they witness the quality of your friendships, they will aspire to have the same. As you mature, your time for friends can become limited, but your impact should expand. It's no longer about how often you hang with your friends; it's about how deep the communication of friendship is when you do. When you make the decision to have fewer friends and more effective friendships, you will become the person you always wanted to be.

Habits

It would be too easy to fall into old habits of our upbringing. People tend to either revert back to their childhood memories as a way of avoiding certain circumstances or run toward them, even if they are unhealthy. Over the course of time your friends will mirror you or you will mirror them. Which reflection is currently the strongest? Typically, there is a mutual reflection from both. Friends are going to have different paths with their choices in career, family, lifestyle, and countless other walks of life.

Develop the habit of friendship dash decisions. We don't need to walk the same exact path as all our friends or vice versa. Friends guide us on a path of success or destruction. Having options lets us choose the path with doing some math, by adding the right influences and subtracting the negative people.

The same way we form habits through repetition, we need to form friendships through trust. Trust is one of the necessary ingredients for any significant relationship to thrive. When you develop trusting relationships you are able to bounce back from adversity much quicker. Having the right people to trust, will instruct you on the right way to live.

Plan

If you desire to have healthy friendships, then there must be a plan. Those who don't have a plan, life happens *to* them. Those who do have a plan, life happens *for* them. Build a dream team of supporters who have your best interest. Develop a circle of trust, with individuals who are truthful and loyal. Think of the most important characteristics you desire in your friendships and seek those qualities in others. Make the decision to limit the influence of those who could be holding you *back*, even if you go way *back* with them. Friendships who share your vision empower you to live your purpose. When purpose is accomplished for one, it is achievable for many. When one friend is winning all their friendships become winners with them.

Sometimes we plan too much time on insignificant things. If you spend more time planning on what you're going to post on social media, than you do your friendships, then you aren't ready for meaningful friendships. It's better to be liked by one person in reality, than liked by a million on Facebook.

Counselor

If you are a caring individual, it can become quite easy to go from being someone's friend to their counselor. At times we will council friends on how to make better decisions and encourage one another during challenging seasons of life. To council them is not bad, to be their counselor is to no longer be their friend. When you become the counselor or counselee the dynamic of the relationship is changed. Counselors can be found anywhere, but friendship is truly a gift. If your friend constantly comes to you with problems and you find yourself drained and dreading spending time with them, the friendship dynamic is shifting.

Sometimes friends become emotionally dependent on you. It is up to you to put up a boundary, not a barrier. This doesn't mean not letting them talk about their problems, but a boundary of referring them to receive professional help from a counselor. Sometimes the best support is to encourage professional help instead of personal advice. The architect of friendship is to build bridges, not walls.

Let your hurting friends know you love them too much to be their counselor, that would much rather be their friend. Also, inform them you are there as a listening ear and a caring heart. Help them to understand it's not that you care any less about the struggle they are going through. On the contrary, you care so much that you hate to see them remain in their current dark place. Don't allow the friendship and counselor role to be confused. Having appropriate boundaries will provide you with appropriate relationships. You can be the positive and supportive friend and provide advice without having to be a counselor. Know when to counsel and when to get back to being friends. This doesn't make you care*less*; it makes you care*ful* in preserving the friendship.

On the opposite end of the spectrum, take the time to evaluate if you are the "friend" constantly seeking advice. You might have slipped into the role of pursuing a counselor instead of a friend. You might actually think the friend who is a good listener is an excellent friend, but in reality, they have been an excellent counselor. Friendships are designed for us to take turns carrying the load for one another. If one person continuously carries the burdens of another, then the friendship is one-sided. When you seek out your friend's time to talk only about yourself, the other person may feel resentful. Refuse to become a client, friendships are meant to be mutual. Each of you should be sharing hopes, fears and laughs while doing life together.

What Are You Living For?

Early in friendships, it's usually common interests that bring friends together. There reaches a point when friends seek out deeper meaning than fun activities. Some friends, mature years ahead of us, while sometimes we mature years ahead of them. Tension begins to mount because one friend is striving for greatness, while the other is content remaining the same. Simply put, some people are in a different season of life. Some are in suffering while others are receiving blessings. Some have a family while others are searching. Some are broke while others have been careful with their money. Some are sober, some are on drugs. As the path widens, the gap in the friendship widens as well.

The question to ask in friendship, is why? You need to know your why. Why do you have chosen those friends? Why is friendship important to you? Why do you allow certain people in and keep others at a distance? When you know the why, you will gain clarity about your next steps.

FRIENDSHIP DASH - PART II

"A true friend is someone who thinks that you are a good egg even though he knows that you are slightly cracked"

Bernard Meltzer

Build Friendships

"People come into your life for a reason, a season or a lifetime"

-Unknown

Any strong relationship isn't built in a day. Have a clear grasp of the seasonal friends. Seasonal friends are the ones who you might have been friends with for years, but you are slowly drifting apart because your vision and priorities have shifted. Those who are meant to stay in your life will make a conscious effort to remain in it for a lifetime. Those who don't will give excuses as to why it's so difficult to hang out. Some friends are there temporarily to teach you a life lesson and then the both of you go your separate ways. Some seasons are short while others remain intact for decades. Other friendships are meant for specific reasons. Taking the time to think about season, reason and lifetime friendship causes you to analyze the importance of each. All three are necessary and will play an important role during your dash.

To Do and Not to Do

Some friends will be inspiring but all friendships need to be. You don't have to find the world's greatest professional or guru to gain wisdom. Sometimes you only need to look at your circle of friends. Others will show you how to live while others show you what not to do, both are equally valuable. While one friend can show you the right path, the next friend can deceive you in believing the wrong path is the correct path. Know your values and don't waver. Friendship will influence you in healthy and unhealthy decision making. For those friends falling on hard times are valuable life lessons to teach you how to avoid similar heartache if possible. Those who have fallen into darkness can't guide you to the light. Those who have found the light can shield you from the darkness. When one person discovers their significance, every person they know moves one step closer to finding theirs.

The Gap

I recently listened to a man talking about how his friendships evolved over time. In his speech he talked about fame, success, fatherhood, marriage and living out the purpose designed for his life. For him to reach his potential, a shift had to happen in his relationships. He had some close friends and family members he attempted to bring on the path to success with him. These individuals attempted to follow in his footsteps. Suddenly, they quickly fell back into old habits. He had been friends with them since they were young, which made his decision more difficult. He loaned them money and jumpstarted their music careers by giving them the opportunity of a lifetime. What he described next was the concept of what happens when friendships stop developing and fall into a rut.

He called this shift, the "GAP". Because of his fame and success, he elevated to a whole new life, and there was a huge gap between him, and the ones he grew up with. As he kept excelling in his passions and purpose, he raised his standards sky high and was determined to make himself a better man. While the gap between him and his friends widened, he continued to rise, while they stayed the same.

In situations where you feel you are increasing your life with healthy choices and relationships; the GAP, cannot be you going back down to their level because you would be required to lose progress. The gap needs to be your circle of friends raising their standard through healthy choices and relationships to catch you. The more you follow your purpose and make positive life changes, the higher you raise your peace and happiness. Invite them on the journey with you. If they are destined to take a ride with you, everyone will reach new heights together. Some friends just go along for the ride, but they aren't willing to close the gap. Some gaps can be reduced other's need to remain at a distance.

Leaving people behind isn't really about leaving them in your past. It's more about leaving behind the old you, to grow into the new you. We all have gaps in our friendships, the narrower they become the deeper they develop. Coach and teach them if they are willing to close the gap. Give them an opportunity to rise with you. If your friends choose not to grow then it's time for you to go, go or grow, those are the options. Set boundaries and communicate clearly what your expectations are. When there is lack of effort, the best approach is to lovingly confront the other person. When words don't match actions, friendships begin to fade away. It's okay to be different than your friends, but not if the difference is dragging you down. Choose wisely which differences divide and which compliment your uniqueness.

friENDship

True friendships last until one person reaches the other side of their dash. Even then, the impact of the friendship can be felt for generations. I think an important question to ask, is if I met this person for the first time in my life, would I seek them out to become my close or best friend? If the answer is no, indicate why you said no. And if you said yes, then seek more of your YES Friendships and leave the NO friends alone.

Recently, I asked many of my friends what the 3 most important things they need in friendship are. As you can imagine I received numerous different answers. These answers ranged from love, respect, loyalty, to encouragement, accountability, and many others. The bottom line is each friend needed something different and we need something different as well. Your personal answer reveals your need. Learning the three biggest needs of your chosen family members, and revealing yours, will reinforce the friendship. When you share your needs, you communicate your standards. The higher you raise your standards the more clarity and excellence will happen in your friendships.

4, 5, 6

"You are the average of the five people you spend the most time with"
Jim Rohn

This simple math adds value and multiplies your quality of life. We all have a team of people in life that we recruit intentionally or passively. If the selected people are not good team players than the math equation subtracts your dreams and divides your relationships. The average five people you choose to spend time and interact with reflects who you are. Think of your five most important friendships and seek more opportunities to invest time with them. With unhealthy friendships or no friendships, your relational well-being is extremely unhealthy, which can turn your solid 5, into a lonely 1.

Really think about those fabulous 5 in your life. Whether you want to believe it or not, they are pushing you in a certain direction. Let them know when you are being pushed in the wrong direction. If they are pushing you in the right direction, then enjoy the ride. By being specific about your team of 5, your possibilities expand, and your limitations are reduced. For those of you who are more social and those of you who are more reserved, the total number varies. The number can be greater than 5 or fewer than 5. Overall, find the number that best works in your life to have the greatest impact possible.

To have a friendship, you must be willing to show friendship. 5 is not huge number in terms of quantity, but it is monstrous in terms of quality. Would you rather have 50 pennies or 5 dimes? The amount is the same but the value of the 5 dimes is more significant than the 50 pennies. 5 dimes are more valuable because they don't require the same amount of stress as trying to carry 50 pennies. Count the cost of your friendships as well as the value. Carrying 50 pennies in your pocket is a burden and 5 dimes is a blessing.

Sometimes less is more and more is less. During certain seasonal dash moments, you will need to make your circle smaller in order for the circle to be stronger. Lastly, remember not everyone IN your circle is actually FOR your circle.

If the statement is true about being the sum total of the 5 people, we spend most of our time with, then let's be honest with ourselves. What is holding you back from making some mid-game substitutions in the game of life? Your starting 5 on the basketball court of influence will not always have the best fit for what your goal is. If you put 5 centers on the court, the team will be sloppy. If you put 5 point guards on the floor you won't be strong enough. Each person who is positioned in your life serves a purpose. Some compliment you while others limit the impact of the team.

You are the captain of your own team in selecting your friend squad. Choose wisely. You have the ability to choose who you put on the floor with you until the end of your life. There will be times when substitutions are necessary, and some of your closest teammates move on to play their game somewhere else. When was the last time you did a scouting report on your team? Closely evaluating the strengths and limitations of those on your team will allow you to become a winner at life. By making the correct substitutions and releasing players who are all about themselves, and adding a team player, you now can become a champion. Champions have the right team by having the right individuals who play the right role for the friendship team.

Helpful Outcome

It is almost impossible to constantly be surrounded by positive influences and still make negative unhealthy choices. So much of your influence comes from those you invest your time in. If you are headed in the wrong direction, I would be willing to bet that your friends are also. Heading in the wrong direction or right direction is a choice typically made by the individual, however, the influence of friendships are undeniable. Many of life's foolish choices were made in the company of other fools. Consequently, many of life's greatest decisions were made with great people.

People, who are successfully adding purpose to their dash, don't give credit to having friends who are heading down the wrong path. The contrary is true. People give credit to those around them who are supportive, encouraging and pursuing their dash as well. The outcome of your purpose is made up of those who poured into your life, allowing you to pour out your passion and talents for the world to see.

Check

A friend should be willing to check on you. If you have suffered from a hardship financially, relationally, or any other endeavor, a real friend will keep it real, even if things are real uncomfortable. The same way you would check your Facebook account, you should be checking on your friends. By being consistent in a quick check up, you develop a level of respect, which every human being desires. The check doesn't have to be long or detailed, but it must be sincere. Friends who say they are "alright" and "fine" might not always be truthful. This could be the moment when they need you to check on them the most. Look beyond the words they are saying and recognize the words they are leaving out. Be a real friend by checking on them regularly. The more checks you deposit, the greater the balance of that friendship.

Accountable

"A friend loves at all times"
Proverbs 17:17 NIV

"Friends won't ever judge, just simply love, no matter the circumstances. Who will be the one to tell you you're slacking in a certain area of your life? Yes, it comes from haters, but I am not talking about the haters, I'm talking about those loved ones who tell us, not because they are haters, they just hate to see us waste our time. Who is bold enough to tell you that you are a workaholic or you're not being there for your spouse and children the way you should be? Who will tell you that your drinking and spending habits are damaging your life and those who care about you? Who will confront the addiction, and negative habits you continue to do? Who will speak up and tell you when you have been untrustworthy, or you are simply being a jerk? What friend will provide you with resources to help you with any challenges you are currently facing whether it's your weight or unemployment? Who will guide you spiritually? WHO????

You need to be secure enough in your own life that you can willingly accept constructive criticism. Those friends, who appear harsh, might just be what the doctor ordered. Sure, it might be a difficult pill to swallow. Sometimes an overdose of reality is better than a dose of "nice". The pill of accountability can be suffocating to the ego, but provide oxygen in the hardest of times. Only when we are confronted, can we see what we were once blinded by. Seek out the friend who will give you the harsh reality instead of the comforting lies.

Search

Generally, when people seek out a spouse, they are looking for specific qualities that attract them to another person. The person we pursue will have certain characteristics that cause us to want to surround ourselves with them by giving them our time. However, that is not the case with our friends. We don't intentionally and strategically choose who we will invest our time with. I believe we should have a similar approach to having friends. Don't just accidentally become best friends with someone because they are cool. Don't be besties because they are popular rich or pretty. Real friendships will expose fake people. Superficial friends, never last only genuine friendships will. An ounce of intentional friendships prevents a gallon of passive aggravation.

The truth is we are all one friend away from radically changing our lives forever. Think of the people you admire, respect, and your role models. What is it about them that make you look up to them? GO and pursue the characteristics they possess. Develop friendships with people of character. Those characteristics you strongly admire can be birthed into your lifestyle when you replace toxic friends with healing friendships. Every other relationship, especially our family improves from our purposeful friendships.

With the intentional increase of pursuing purpose, you come closer to the razor's edge of advantage. Purpose was never meant to be consumed; it was designed to be shared and spread like a wildfire. As one candle is lit, it should be passed on to light another. Now we are all burning with passion because one decided to spread their purpose. Get vision, and then share vision so there is one less blind person in the world. We are all one friendship away from a radically transformed dash.

Future Friendship

Friendships provide uncomfortable challenges as well as encouraging comfort. To understand friendship, you need to seek out your own definition of friendship. In your best friendship, the other person should bring the BEST out of you. That is where the term best friend comes from. This person is the best person to help you become the best version of you. BEST friends push you toward greatness. Whenever you have someone's best, you too also become your best, impacting others to do their best. If the person you call best friend doesn't help you become the best person in all your other roles, they are not your best friend. There's a difference between close friends and best friends. Close friends can be those you spend the most time with. Best friends are the ones who you invest the best time with. Your best friend can and should inspire you to grow deeper spiritually, become a better spouse, parent, and person. You wouldn't want your ship to be guided by a mediocre captain, so why would you let mediocre friends guide your life?

Purpose

"As iron sharpens iron so one person does for another"
Proverbs 27:17 NIV

If you were in a hospital and you had to receive a heart transplant, would you want a doctor who specializes in heart transplants or a foot doctor? I think the answer is so obvious it's almost stupid. Without having the right people in your circle to help you complete the mission in life you are pursuing, you will become distracted with those who are going in a different direction. Associating with the wrong doctor or friends can even cause further health concerns. In the book of Proverbs, a scripture mentions the importance of having the necessary people in your life to guide you towards your destiny.

A blade is sharpened by rubbing a smooth edge against a rough edge. These rough edges represent people meant to rub away those things in our lives that are not in sync with our destiny. Their wisdom is to be sought after like a lost treasure. You can find the lost treasure when you interact and build relationships with those who are further ahead on the journey. Friendships are the satellite signals sent by God to guide you towards the ultimate destination. Having more GPS's will improve your efficiency of reaching your desired destination.

With the intentional increase of pursuing purpose, you come closer to the razor's edge of advantage. Purpose was never meant to be consumed; it was designed to be shared and spread like a wildfire. As one candle is lit, it should be passed on to light another. Now we are all burning with passion because one decided to spread their purpose. Get vision, and then share vision so there is one less blind person in the world.

Perfect Love

The love that we all truly desire is perfect love. This love isn't, circumstantial, or situational. You can't earn it or and you don't deserve it. This love is a free gift and your effort and accomplishments have nothing to do with receiving it. Jesus loves us enough to love us just the way we are. At the same time, He loves us enough to not let us stay the same. Friendship should emulate the love of Christ. This type of love and friendship are rare and should never be wasted. Jesus willingly laid down his life to die for all of us; not just believers, good people, church goers, tithers, pastors. He died for the addict, the abused, the neglected, lonely, broke and criminals. He died for everyone; no exceptions. He didn't die more for one person, race, religion, sexual orientation, and gender more than another. You will feel the unfailing love of a friendship. You are only one friendship away from the greatest friendship of all time.

Friendship Dash Goals

Identify 2 healthy friendships you have or identify 2 people you can develop healthy friendships with over the next 30 days.

Identify 1 friend that you need to limit your time with over the next 30 days.

1)_____

2)_____

3)_____

FUN DASH -

"People rarely succeed unless they have fun in what they are doing"
Dale Carnegie

Fun should be purposeful, and bring out the best in all of us. Where there is fun, there is learning, if we take the time to evaluate the fun. The learning could be physical activity, teamwork, challenging yourself or breaking out of your comfort zone. Even your relationships are more fulfilled when fun is included. The brain tends to function better when you are engaged in activities you deem to be meaningful and energizing. When you are in a funk, you usually aren't having fun. When you choose fun, you experience a taste of excitement and positivity. Fun is a stress reliever and helps you develop coping skills. Fun is the frosting to your cake and without it, life simply isn't as delicious.

Go ahead and do something you have never done before. Have some purposeful pleasure by knowing you have limited time for enjoyment and refuse to wait another moment to make it happen. Attempt the unknown, dare to forget about making money today, for tomorrows bills.

Children simply have more fun than adults do. Adults lose their sense of fun when they have too many draining responsibilities, and not enough fulfilling fun to provide the balance. Children are living the good life. It's no fair! I want to have more fun than children, and deep down inside, so do you. No responsibility should ever stop you from having a life worth living. It's your responsibility to have fun and you should never be too busy or old to have some. Now's your chance, not tomorrow. Go have fun, until your life is done.

No Fun

Too many unfortunate events have happened to us, preventing us from pursuing fun. Life is now no fun because we are mad at people and circumstances. We figure if we bury ourselves with work, we can avoid all the problems. We begin working really hard, to meet mommy and daddy's expectations until we reach exhaustion to prove we are worthy of approval and respect. Attempting to live up to those expectations and prove our worthiness never fulfills us. In fact reaching those misguided goals can leave us burnt out and more stressed. Trying to be who others want us to be instead of being who we are designed to be removes the opportunity for enjoyment to exist. We all have our reasons as to why having fun isn't a priority. Maybe there's no time, money, or we simply forgot how to. Realistically, they are all excuses. Excuses are strategic disguises that claim important reasoning for one's decision. Despite your schedule or unfair circumstances, no matter how challenging life gets, you still can choose to live a fun one.

Don't let another day arrive without making some memories. Take a breath, laugh, smile, and enjoy the simple things. It's never too late to rewrite the future of your history.

Create

You have the option to create new fun. Fun doesn't have to be thousands of dollars spent on a vacation, because even vacations can be ruined by a poor attitude. If the idea of enjoying yourself sounds complicated, recognize there are endless opportunities for entertainment. Fun can be watching a comedy, playing a board game as a family, reading a book, fixing something around the house, volunteering, hiking, and the list goes on. Some of these ideas can be intimidating if they are unfamiliar. Frequently, the fun factor is eliminated due to a deep fear we have. What is something you've always wanted to try, but never did because of fear? Or something adventurous you wanted to pursue, but it was too much money or too risky? Try it anyway! This could be your last opportunity.

I can remember a time when I used to get invited to go camping, and I always said no. The reason was because I had already proclaimed camping wasn't for me, before I even tried it. I thought it was gross, boring and there was nothing to do. Fast forward a few years later and now I go camping every year and can't envision my life without it. There is power in trying something different, new and challenging. Every year as a family we schedule time to go camping together. Trying a perceived boring activity sparingly can turn into inspiring fun regularly. At first, doing something uncomfortable is intimidating, but you will never know what could be, if you always do what you are used to doing. Sure, it will scare you at first and could even appear to be boring, but you know what's even more scary and boring? Never daring to do something scary and boring! What once was labeled as boring and scary soon becomes a tradition for your entire circle. Get creative and think about a new idea that you have procrastinated about trying and go live a little. When you live a little, life becomes a little bigger.

Actually Have Fun

Sure, you can have the car, house, big yard, clothes, jewelry even a beautiful spouse and children, but do you have the time to enjoy them? Learning to say no to some good things, gives you margin to say yes to the best things. Without taking the time to appreciate the gifts you have; your gifts might appear to be a burden instead of a blessing. To live your dash, you must be in a constant bucket list approach to life. Don't have a bucket list? Stop reading right now and make one!

Now that your back, you can move forward. It doesn't matter if the list has one thing on it; at least you were brave enough to make a list. Your bucket could tip over any day and the dash on your tombstone would be one of regret. The greatest regrets in life are not what we did, but what we feared to attempt. What are the memories people will laugh and reflect on when they visit your tombstone? Let that question sink in. Is it possible that you could have been a tiny bit more adventurous? The answer is yes; we all can. Don't wait another day, your time is running out.

Lies

We all hope that people come to our funeral and share the good qualities and times we had together. People will come and share stories and we should hope they are completely honest in their assessment of us. People might say what a hard worker you were, a great family person you were, which can all be true, but did you truly enjoy life. If you knew that today was your last day on earth, could you sincerely say that your life has been exciting?

Did you breathe, relax, and appreciate the present moment? Were you in awe of the sunset-painted sky? Did you feel refreshed from the sunrise hitting the earth? Did you sing and dance like nobody is watching? Did you laugh and take the adventure you always dreamed of? Once you have, there will be a sense of freedom to not seeking approval from others. We fear fun at times because of what others might think. The fear of other's opinions is a hindrance to our enjoyment. Subtract judgmental opinions and add fun goals, and your life will come closer to equaling enjoyment. Being fun- oriented and desiring to make memories that will last a lifetime will cause your perspective to improve. Each day is an opportunity to make a lasting memory; all it takes is the right attitude and the will to experience a dash of fun.

Mistakes

Take time to laugh at your own mistakes and not dwell on them forever. Mistakes can be hazardous or valuable life lessons. They are either the reason we fail or our greatest professor. There is no true mistake if you honestly learned from it. Mistakes should not be viewed as negative, but a necessary stepping stone to success. How you view mistakes will shape your life. Either mistakes are awful and make you miserable, or you can reflect on poor judgment, and be more equipped for your next life decision. Personally, I love mistakes, Yeah, that's right! I love mistakes. The reason I love mistakes is because I get to learn something new! If I am not making mistakes, I am not learning and not growing because I am not being challenged. Saying mistakes are fun sounds insane. However, deciding not to make the same mistake again, sounds like an exciting adventure that we should all sign up for.

Don't be ashamed you made a mistake, be more embarrassed that you never tried hard enough at life to even make one. Failure is a superior teacher, just remain a student and your ability to teach others, will be limitless. Mistakes come prior to wisdom. Wisdom also pertains to how you are entertained. The do's and don'ts of your recreation carries over into other avenues of your life. When fun habits are destructive, your relationships suffer. When they are constructive, your relationships grow. The journey will have challenges, but it is through the hills and valleys you discover your next greatest passion. A fun filled life will have a mix of mistakes and wisdom. Go ahead make mistakes and have fun learning from them.

Fun for Every 1

Fun does not discriminate; it does not have a preference for our background, circumstances or socioeconomic status. If you are a CEO, single parent, 85 years old or disabled, no worries. There is fun for you too. You need to simply make it a priority. Too often, our schedules control us, instead of us, controlling our schedules. People, who take fun seriously, will take that much needed day off of work. A day off is needed so you can best take care of your family, friends and most importantly, yourself. Fun is not an option, it's mandatory if you want to live your dash with purpose. There is something about engaging in entertaining activities that makes us all feel a little bit more alive. How tragic it would be to have decided to live your entire life and have the unmet need of fun. I am not discounting responsibilities; however, your ability to be responsible is quite limited when you have limited your happiness. Any task will be more effective if it's done with a cheerful heart. Schedule some YOU time, so YOU can be the person YOU were meant to be.

Family Fun

Fun doesn't always have to be tradition. Although, family traditions are important for generations, the same tradition can be changed at some point. It's never too late to start a new family tradition of fun. A new tradition can be weekly, monthly or yearly. Investing in fun is investing in relationships. There needs to be a balance on when to make and break tradition. Ask those you love if they are ready for something new. Some may say no; some may say yes. Despite the answers, be bold enough to motivate the doubters to be brave enough to persevere on your current path, or blaze a new trail.

I told my wife years ago, that every year we were going to Disney world. For two years that's what we did, and we enjoyed our time as a family. When the third was approaching, we began to change our idea of what our family tradition should be. We both came to the agreement that we wanted to travel the world and seeing Disney every year would prevent that from happening. Having a travel bucket list can give you extra motivation to explore and see what types of fun exists in other parts of the globe. I am glad the tradition that I desperately loved, changed.

If the tradition hadn't ended, I never would have discovered what new traditions we could have started. We now travel to a new place every year. I like this tradition much better and so does the rest of my family. Maybe Disney will happen again in the future, (probably, by myself). The seasons and reasons for our travel bucket list of fun were full of Disney. We got our fill, and decided to empty the bucket to make room and fill it with other states and countries instead. By stopping the stubbornness of my Disney fever, I was able to take a chance on other opportunities in life, which I am thankful for. But I still do miss Magic Kingdom.

Cup

Imagine you're thirsty, and in need of some water. For you to have your need for thirst met there has to be something in the cup. If the cup is empty, you wouldn't drink from it because there would be nothing left to meet the purpose you are seeking. Can you invest in your marriage, children, career, relationships, friends and/or school, if you are pouring from an empty cup? Of course not! There's nothing to give out and nothing to receive. An empty cup in life is someone who has poured out their time and responsibilities, but never took the time to get a refill. You get a refill by having fun. Go ahead and fill up by dumping out the worries and stress of adulating. Grab a cup and fill it up with an adventure. As soon as you slow down long enough to quench your thirst for excitement, you will be refreshed. When you become refreshed, suddenly your mood improves. Once your mood improves, then your day improves, then your week, month and eventually, your life all receive a much-needed boost. If you want improvement in all your relationships and aspects of life, then take time to fill your cup and stop emptying yourself without the presence of mind to refuel.

Fill your tank of life with memories of fun and stop making excuses. Start taking care of you by being good to yourself. The ability to care for others is limited when you have no time for self-care. Go ahead and take a break. There is a reason the word break is called a break. If you don't take a break, life will break you.

Optimist

The interesting thing about fun is that it's consistent with optimism. A better attitude leaves a better chance at having fun. Just because a situation isn't ideal, doesn't mean fun cannot exist. When the sun is shining its quite easy to have some fun, how about when it rains? Allow the fun to come pouring in. Fun is intentional. When the rain hits you, you have two choices, either drown or grab a life jacket. Allowing insignificant things to steal your happiness is choosing to sink instead of swim.

We all become irritated, but we shouldn't let feelings be the thermostat for our happiness. The unfortunate reality is you have the ability to choose anger, frustration and boredom. The power to choose anger over happiness is a process decided daily. Next time your mad about something, say out loud "I am choosing to be angry and choosing to stay angry." Try it, you will soon see how ridiculous it is to stay angry and let your emotions drain you. Also, declare you are choosing not to have fun because of how you feel. That is awful isn't it? It's normal to be angry and upset but don't live there. It's okay to visit but don't start paying rent. Find the hidden blessing in the current lesson. Don't let any boring person (you included) stop you from a life to explore more, be more, and adventure more.

Fun All Week

When we reach adulthood it's easy to forget about real fun, we experienced at age 10. Life is not all fun and games but sometimes it should be. We can forget what it feels like to simply be free. It's exhausting to have the routine of paying bills, being stressed until you break your hip then die, just kidding, sort of. The same responsibilities we desired when we were young such as driving, having our own money, owning a home are now crippling the possibility of fun. Now that we have the car, money and home all we do is complain about it. Now we want to go back to childhood to rid ourselves of what we desperately longed for. Let's decide to decide on what we really want. The fun things were never found in things, because things eventually disappoint.

Some find fun only certain times a year, or month. *Living for Friday fun,* isn't really fun either. Fun isn't a day of the week or the weekend. It isn't even a circumstance, or activity that you're excited about. Fun is a culture that is Monday through Sunday. It's the ability to see the light during the dark challenges. Fun is a glowing sensation of freedom. Fun is right next to you if you can remain open minded. You never know when the next opportunity of fun will arrive. Keep seeking until you have found fun or fun has found you. True joyful fun isn't found in people, places or things. It's found in a greater purpose greater than anything this world has to offer.

Laugh Now and Laugh Later

By remaining curious about life, it never gets old. Every day is an experience, and everyday experiences bring fun to the journey when we are looking for them. Examples such as getting gas and going to the grocery store can take a whole new meaning when we recognize that any moment something memorable may happen. Running into an old friend, getting a good deal on product, listening to some good music, interacting with people in your community, there are countless opportunities for positivity to leak into your life.

Much of experiencing life is learning how to laugh and finding humor in everyday situations. A while back I was having a difficult day fighting off depression. I was very emotional and didn't have the energy to really do anything. My oldest daughter came up to me and cracked a funny joke. I couldn't help but laugh. Soon as I laughed, I remember feeling a spark in my body. My whole mood shifted a jolt of energy went through my body. My entire perspective radically changed, because of laughter. The depression wasn't at the forefront of my brain and I was able to be optimistic again. Fun is being able to let your heart smile when your face can't. Sharing a good laugh with someone you love can positively impact your mental health. Just think how challenging it is to be depressed, stressed, worried, angry, sad, and upset while you're laughing. Try it sometime, you can't do it! Although, these emotions are normal we aren't meant to stay in the darkness. Laughter brings the bright light to your face and your spirit. Fortunately, you can choose to pursue humor. I dare you to find more reasons to laugh and go find the irony and humor in your circumstances. Choose to celebrate a fun filled party of life instead of a pity party.

FUN DASH - PART II

"When fun gets deep enough it can heal the world"
The Oaqui

Routine

"Be yourself, everyone else is taken"

Oscar Wilde

Sometimes fun is replaced with routine. The 9-5 same old same old happens. The same pattern and habits run your life. Eventually your heart, mind and spirit are begging for change, and something out of the ordinary. When people reflect on their lives they don't say "wow I had such a great routine I'm glad I never changed it". Even the greatest routines need fine tuning periodically. People don't think "I am so thankful I was so boring and predictable and never tried anything new". Nobody says, "I'm so thrilled I didn't pursue my dreams and goals and live life to my fullest potential, and I am so grateful I never attempted anything on my bucket list". NOBODY says that! If they do, run, run far far away. We often stay with the same idea of fun because it's comfortable and keeps us feeling secure. If you do what you have always done, you will never be who you were meant to be.

We can't think about someone else's dreams, or how blessed they are because they chose to live their dash. Thinking about someone else's dash would leave you no room to live yours. Take the time learn a new language, practice that instrument, go to that concert, start that business, study that new skill, finish your education, change your career, just be different. The fun sometimes begins, as soon as the routine ends. We can have a fun routine and it can be memorable, but from time to time just GO! Go do something unique. Just do what you think you can't, and soon you will say I am glad I did.

Try something different and see the possibilities instead of the limitations. A brand-new start will guide you to a superior journey. Until you do something new you will not be renewed. One of the top killers of growth is comfort. Comfort never leads to breakthrough. Do something new, and become the upgraded you.

Here's an example of changing up the routine. Years ago, we were choosing to be bored one day at our house. Instead of remaining in the state of boredom my wife wanted to go somewhere. Going somewhere doesn't necessarily change the boredom, because boredom is a choice. However, sometimes a new environment is needed for a clearer perspective. Now, to go to anywhere we desired to visit we would have to travel several hours. It was then my wife said something I will never forget. She looked at me dead in the eyes and said, New Jersey tomorrow? I looked at her like she was crazy. I thought maybe she was on drugs. But she doesn't do drugs, (but I thought maybe she was smoking something really good). We all have something that gets us high. Her high is traveling and she wanted to get high, real high! I reluctantly joined in her in the madness. The next day we got in our car and drove 7 hours to visit family and had the trip of a lifetime.

That is the bucket list approach to life, and I am so thankful that I was forced out of my comfort zone.

I know what you're thinking, the Cruz family is insane! You would partially be right in your assessment. You are also probably thinking, taking a trip like that is unrealistic because of work, kids, school, pets, sports, meetings, responsibilities and all that stuff. It's not always realistic to travel hundreds or thousands of miles in a moment sporadically. There is always something you can do to change things up. I would suggest that one random weekend when your family has nothing planned just LEAVE! Or if you're like most families and you always have something planned put up a boundary to the rest of the world and learn the word NO. Say no to others and say yes to your family. That means leave some margin in your life and calendar to have the ability to do something random and memorable. Yes, that's right go somewhere go on a short drive a few hours away to somewhere you have never been, or go on a short flight. Take a road trip to a state or national park or a city you have always wanted to see. Go do something even if its 1 hour away or 2 or 3 or 27. Take a drive to explore and come back the same night if you have to. Ultimately, for the excitement to begin, you need to be brave enough to discover freedom through adventure.

Adults are Boring

Some people feel guilty about enjoying life, so they criticize others for having too much fun. One of the ways our family pursues our fun dash is that we are passionate about traveling. Instead of hearing people ask us about vacations and appreciating the beauty of adventure, we are sometimes received with criticism. Some of the frequent comments we hear are "Must be nice to travel all the time" "You guys are always traveling" "Where are you going this week?" "When are you guys going to slow down? Those are just some of the sarcastic comments and questions I have heard while enjoying my life.

Don't take it personal when you live your dash, people will question you and try to make you feel terrible for pursuing your goals because they simply never pursued theirs. They essentially have become your biggest fans disguised as your critics. They are behind the scenes wishing they could laugh, love, and live a fulfilled life that you already have made a reality. Unfortunately, people want to see other's struggle. If other's see you doing well, they have to make sure you aren't doing better than they are. The more haters you have, the more likely you are living a dash that people desire. I feel zero guilt about seeing the world with my wife and children and you shouldn't feel any either.

reTIRE

Maybe we have heard our parents or friends who talk about retirement. They may have an excellent plan for the future but what about the possibility of not making it to retirement? That is always a realistic scenario. You might not make it to the old age to retire and start to live, you must start living now. Some become so tired they won't make it to retire. Working almost your entire life to possibly stay healthy and take a break is grueling. Deep inside of your being, you desire to live your dash in a manner where people think your living in retirement right now! I know this is a high standard, but life isn't designed to be mediocre. Opportunities of once in a lifetime can happen once a day, not once in a lifetime. You can either choose to be bold or be boring, you can't do both. Discover what you love and do what you love with those you love. Retire from being old, the old you, and replenish your body with fun. I promise it won't hurt, well maybe a little at first, but it's worth it.

Think Back

I can remember specific times as a child saying I'm bored. Now as an adult, I am older and have learned to whine differently. When I'm bored, instead of saying "I'm bored," as adults, we check social media looking for a nice ego boost with likes and comments to decrease our boredom levels. Social media is our way to improve our mood because we are bored. This tactic doesn't remove the boredom it just temporarily delays it until we get our next notification.

Adults declare boredom by working too many hours and staying "busy". We overschedule because we feel we will miss out if we say no to others. We don't want to say no because we want to feel wanted. Being wanted makes us feel good and feeling good will help us not feel bored anymore, so we say yes, and overschedule and stress out our family just to not be bored. If we aren't careful our immature habits from childhood will follow us into adulthood.

New Stuff

We are never satisfied and always want something new. We want a new car, house, job, wardrobe, and a new phone. We want, want and want because it's new, new and new. If we knew how much new actually costs. We want knew because old is boring. The challenge is that everything eventually gets old. Once something is old it's no fun anymore. We not only do this with our stuff but even out relationships! Take the time to appreciate the old so it stays new in your mind. Be more concerned with a new you, rather than a new thing.

Rain Dance

I remember a specific time during the summer when my children were younger; they were about ages 7 and 5. It was a beautiful summer day and all of a sudden it started to downpour. My wife looked at all of us and said let's go play in the rain (once again, I thought she was on drugs). I was thinking, why would we intentionally go outside while it's down pouring? We refused to let the rain reign over our fun. We all put on our bathing suits and ran outside in the rain for a few minutes. For the first time in my adulthood I remembered the sense of aww and wonder of being a child again. In all of my life I have never enjoyed the rain as much as I did in that moment, because I didn't allow the rain to change the pursuit of my dash. We chose to enjoy in the middle of a storm, literally! I often think about that simple, yet precious memory. In that moment, I reflected and thought, I can't believe we are doing this, but I am thrilled that we are. Go dance in the rain with your family at least one time in your life. I promise it will be a lifelong memory. Fun is important, it is being in the middle of a rain storm and instead of whining you put on your bathing suit and dance in the rain.

Sloth

We are familiar with the sloth; a very slow-moving animal. The sloth moves so slow algae and fungi start to grow on its body. They are so slow and comfortable that disgustingness lives on them. Take a break from the Netflix and get off the couch. When we compare our success to others further along, it's too easy to think our progress is like a sloth. Even if we move like a sloth, at least we are moving. There will be tough times when not moving feels like our only option. Your reason must be stronger than your season. Some seasons are slow. Some are fast paced. Either way we should move at least one step in the direction of progress. We aren't all meant to be cheetahs, but we are all designed to get moving.

Best Day of My Life Again

About a year ago, we went on an adventurous hiking trip. On the hike we discovered a location where you can literally slide down a waterfall like a water slide. How cool is that? During our excursion we were able to bring our nephew with us. At first, he was terrified. He was determined that he would not go down the waterfall slide. He was shaking with fear. Too bad for him, I am bigger and stronger than he is. I didn't really care about his comfort zone, so I decided he was going. After I forced him, (I mean kindly asked him to go with me) he said yes. Once the fear was conquered, we celebrated together. Once I was able to trick him into having fun, the rest of the trip was much better. After we finished up waterfall sliding my nephew said, "This was the most fun day of my life." This was the third time he had said this to us in less than a year. That doesn't make his statement insincere, it's rather intriguing. The most fun day of your life doesn't have to happen only once. It can happen several times over and over again. When you become exposed to new experiences you can advance your idea of fun.

Don't Judge Fun

One's personal definition of fun is completely different from the next person. You often think that your idea of fun is somehow better than someone else's idea of fun. Their fun isn't boring or wrong, it is simply different than yours. Don't try to live up to the expectations of someone else's fun, discover your own and don't judge the next person's. All those people you think are boring, they are thinking the same thing about some of the stuff that you do. Fun is subjective and is not one size fits all. Since you are unique, your concept of fun is also unique. Now go ahead, and have the most fun day of your life all over again.

Fun Tired

Your fun activities will shift and become old, and no longer thrilling. This is the fun-fatigue and yes, it is real. It comes from doing the same thing over and over again. When you repeat, sometimes the seasoning spice of life becomes dull. This is normal. Don't freak out. Sometimes that one exciting thing is boring because you are maturing. You have matured enough to try something new, and once again you will be pulled out of your comfort zone. A red flag of fun-fatigue could be from being too stressed or depressed and nothing is fun anymore.

So how do you know the difference between fun-fatigue and depression? Fun-fatigue will cause you to take a break and explore other options. You will seek out new fun in a new activity, leaving the old activity behind. When you are depressed and don't allow yourself to enjoy life, you have stopped your favorite activities and haven't replaced them with anything. You remain bored, and having fun becomes a foreign concept. Those events that used to excite you and left you drooling with anticipation, now leave you feeling worried and worn out. Constantly check yourself, and see if you are slipping into a dark period of life or you are simply maturing to something greater. When you drift away from having fun, exhaustion is sure to follow. We all become tired, when you become tired, let it be from having a significant amount of fun; don't let it be from something dreadful.

Put the FUN in FUNeral

I am excited for the quality of my dash to impact others when my funeral arrives. Live in a manner in which people are celebrating the life you lived. Let other's cheer on your greatness. Let the funeral be a time of honor, love, respect and reminiscent of good times.

If you had to pick a song that reminds you of your story what would it be? What is the theme song to your life? If you could pick a song that summarizes your life, goals, hopes, and dreams what song would it be? The song stuck in your head from childhood doesn't have to be the same song forever. When you change your mind you change your path, giving you a whole new song to share with the world. The theme song for your life can be a compass that casts a vision of the path you're on, or the road you intend to take. My theme song is called One day too Late by Skillet. What's yours? Don't have one? Search for one right now. Find a song that embodies the life you desire to live.

I also have a funeral song. Yes, you read that correctly. I have a song already picked out that I want played at my funeral, sounds creepy doesn't it? When you take the time to choose a funeral song you develop a more valuable perspective on life. My funeral song is called *"Home"* by Chris Tomlin. The song is a perfect song to send me off to my final destination. I hope everyone sings loud and proud and has some fun at my FUNeral. Turn the music up find a theme song for your life, and a funeral song to be remembered by. Allow the power of music to add to your dash and inspire others to pursue their legacy.

Make a Choice

The tears of sorrow happen because there are no tomorrows. Tears of joy occur when there is hope for infinite tomorrows. When you choose to seriously have fun, you can motivate others to live presently, and change the path of their tomorrows. Want to have fun? Know who you are, and where you are going. If tomorrow doesn't come, what a ride it has been.

What is it you are waiting for? You have been dying for change; or you have been dying slowly inside because you have chosen to stay the same. A change that will positively impact your life should never have to wait another breath. With all that was covered in this chapter, any strategy of avoiding the fun you so desperately need, would be nothing but an excuse to be boring. You will either be bored or be having fun, which sounds better to you?

Fun Dash Goals

Identify 3 new activities or adventures that you will start
planning for and follow through on over the next 30 days.

1)_____

2)_____

3)_____

FINANCE DASH -

It's simple arithmetic. Your income can grow only to the extent that you do.

Harv Eker

Your dash will be costly, but your life is priceless. Your life and the decisions you make lead you towards financial freedom or leave you trapped in poverty. Like it or not, we all need money. Money is not evil; it is the love of money that is evil. (1 Timothy 6:10) Money is also not good, it's neutral. What gives money its importance, is the value we place on it. It's how we view the money that influences our decisions. Money won't bring you happiness but a lack of it can also bring crisis. Finances, like any other object in life can be used for positive and negative purposes. The power of money will either limit your options or expand your opportunities. Use money foolishly and watch it go, or use it wisely and watch it grow.

Relationship

We have relationships with our spouse, children and friends; however, we also have a relationship with money. Any relationship can be draining or refueling. It depends on how the relationship is managed. Some relationships are experiencing growth, while others remain strenuous from neglect. What is your current relationship status with your finances? Are you single, married, happily married, dating, engaged or divorced? These terms are all being used metaphorically. However, they are necessary to assess a relational management of finances. When others bring up money do you get nervous and never speak? Are you quick to talk about money? How you respond when the topic of finances is brought up in conversation indicates the kind of relationship you have with your finances. The more excited you are to talk about money, the more likely the healthier the relationship you have with money. The quieter and more uncomfortable you become when discussing money represents a red flag. This could mean the relationship with money has been damaged and silence is a way of avoidance. Or for some people they are sick and tired of every conversation being about money and they simply want a break. Finding the balance in knowing when to engage and when space is needed, is crucial to relationships with people and discussing finances. Ultimately, your relationship with money needs to be nurtured like any other human relationship.

For some individuals, the idea of talking about spending, saving, giving, investing, budgeting is taboo and should be kept quiet. Everyone has their own approach on how to talk or not talk about finances. It's intriguing to discover that relational and financial well-being is directly linked. When there are money problems, typically relationship problems aren't far behind. The mismanagement of finances leads to mismanaged relationships. Being committed in your finances provides stability and a track record to keep the rest of your commitments. People are as reliable as their commitments. Committed people are more likely to be committed to financial growth.

Money is a test of character and responsibility. If you waste money, you waste time, and if you waste time, you waste your relationships. Make a conscious decision to improve your relationship status with money. Your relationship status with money indicates how healthy your relationships will become. If your financial habits are unstable and unhealthy, your relationships tend to be similar. When you take your financial health seriously, your relationships with everyone you know will begin to grow.

How We Do Things

I know quite a few people who believe my family is rich and loaded with tons of money. This couldn't be further from the truth, since when I go to the grocery store, I still wonder if my debit card will be declined (Just kidding). People perceive us to be wealthy because we have been known to take frequent family vacations. I don't believe this makes us wealthier than anyone else. Vacations have been a priority for my family. We believe it's very important to get away as a family and make memories. Ironically, some of the individuals who have labeled us as having a ton of money actually make more money than we do!

We aren't materialistic and don't need the latest trends. We don't have any car payments and drive a 2007 Toyota Camry and 2005 Honda Pilot. We have a budget that we follow. We donate 10 % to our church and other organizations; we save 15 % into investment accounts such as mutual funds, IRA's 401k's and 403B's, these accounts that are like savings accounts on steroids. If you are unaware on how the accounts work or how to open one, I would recommend that you research financial advisors in your community.

We live off 75% of our income. We believe if we can't live off 75% then we are living out of our means. I am not saying go and try that today. That requires planning and a well-organized system that is developed over time. I would suggest with only living on 90% of your income to begin with, and then make adjustments from there as needed. Create a budget of all income with all expenses. This will cast the vision for your financial future and present circumstances. Without a budget you won't have a plan. Without a plan you will continue to struggle. Everyone's situation is different, but not having a budget is about as smart as taking your driver's test with a blind fold on. You are asking for a disaster. Go ahead and make some small preparations and see the bigger picture. Even small preparations have huge results.

Make It Take It

An extremely important concept regarding finances is not how much money you make; it's how much you keep. If not managed properly, the more you make, the more the government takes. The more you make, the more you spend. This is a typical cycle of the relationship with money that we have all endured at some point. The right cycle of income versus outcome is to have higher incoming money and less outgoing money; a simple but difficult concept to bring into reality. Without planning, money disappears much faster than you earn it. With discipline, your money will outlast your life and carry on to your children and grandchildren. If you have any desire to improve the quality of life for your loved ones, then start by having self-control. The one habit of discipline can change a family tree forever. If you want your checks to last longer than the month, then learn the magic word and just say NO to unnecessary things. This happens with an intentional decision to not be stupid with money. Choosing to not be stupid is pretty smart.

Strategize

Some common ways to adjust your finances to live a comfortable life include lowering your cell phone bill, cutting cable costs, refinancing your home, go out to eat less and bring lunches to work. Be brave and ask for that raise, cancel the credit cards and pay down some debt. Utilize the skills and opportunities you have to improve your financial situation. Employment is a great resource to add to your wealth, but not at the sacrifice of your health. Don't work yourself into stress and out of happiness. Find work you truly enjoy, and you will already be rich. Don't spend more time on building up your organization than relationships with your family. The greater blessing is to love your purposeful work and still make sure that your family knows you love them more.

If you feel like you're dumb with money, that's okay, you aren't the only one. I have spent decades being stupid with money. Congratulations! There is a way to combat stupidity. It's called education. Learn from smart people. Hire a financial advisor and other financially-savvy individuals. Reading finance books by Dave Ramsey will change your financial situation for life if you apply his 7-step process. My family's financial situation has changed for life by simply following his financial wisdom. Some specific finance books that will change your finance dash are *Financial Peace, Total Money Makeover, Rich Dad Poor Dad, Think and Grow Rich.*

Study specific finance professionals and learn some of their principles such as Clark Howard, Tony Robbins, Warren Buffet, and Robert Kiyosaki. Websites such as money.com, pennyhoarder.com, Investopedia.com, nerdwallet.com, and countless others, provide tips and advice on how to change your financial relationship. Without taking the time to seek out finance opportunities, you will be hiding from bill collectors. Instead of hiding from creditors, why not seek financial education and graduate to financial stability.

Live and Give

Some people live for money, others die for it, and some are even willing to kill for it. Maybe not always literally, but people are dying each day they sacrifice happiness for the almighty dollar. They are killing themselves by sacrificing peace and time with their family to chase a dream, not realizing life without those you love is a nightmare. How could something such as paper or plastic cause us to be willing to sacrifice our lives for it? Finances are never worth the stress that's placed on your body. Having money is needed, and striving to obtain it is important. Let's face it, without our finances in order; our life is out of order. Life is short; don't make it shorter by trying to work longer hours. Too much stress and time at work leads too much less quality time at life. Don't die trying to make a living.

I DARE YOU

I am going to challenge you. Take one dollar and give it away! Seriously, try it. If you have the power to give money away to help others, money won't ever have the power over you. If we aren't careful, we all can become prisoners to something. If you can't give money away to help meet the needs of other's, you don't own the money, the money owns you! If you don't want to be a prisoner to something, set it free, you set money and yourself free by giving it to someone who needs it more than you. There is nothing more freeing, than to free oneself while freeing others. When you give you are one step closer to wealthy pockets and rich hearts when you break the chains of greed and are healed with generosity.

Money is a powerful tool to your dash, especially when it's being used generously. The more you give, the more you live. People aren't remembered for how much money they kept to themselves, their legacy is reflected in how much they gave to others.

An example in my own personal life is one time we were low on money and we had been faithful in our giving. Something amazing happened. We came home one day after being gone for several hours to randomly find an envelope, inside the envelope was $500, we were shocked and thankful. Wow, what a blessing to receive that gift randomly! But not really randomly, since I can give countless examples on how

163

giving has always brought us financial gains, not only financial gains but personal growth. We believe giving is extremely important, and God will be faithful and take care of us. We have always received more than we have ever given. Giving is like interest at a bank, the more money you put into the bank, the more you earn on interest. The more you give away, the more is given back to you. Now that is a deal! Anyone have any interest, on making some interest?

Circle of Money

If we aren't careful, we can adopt some broke habits from our broke friends. Having poor habits is done with no effort. Having rich habits can only be done intentionally. We often associate with others who are on a similar financial path as we are. Wealthy people have wealthy friends, and broke people have broke friends. It might sound harsh, but that's reality. If we are in financial hardship or financial blessing, we socialize with those who we can relate with financially.

I have a couple questions that can help this theory. How many millionaires do you know? How many millionaires do you know who have other wealthy friends? How many broke people do you know? How many broke people do you know who have broke friends? Wealth rubs off on people the same way being broke rubs off on people. Healthy habits are contagious and spread fast. Unhealthy habits spread even faster. Be careful about which habits you inherit from your circle of influence. Expand your circle with knowledge of wealth building and witness the circle grow together in financial freedom. One by one, those closest to you are guided towards financial freedom or financial bondage.

Stuff

Most people desire more money but won't make sacrifices to achieve it. Do you really need the latest iPhone, Jordan's, new car with the new car payment, big television, expensive clothes? They may all bring a façade of having an excellent status symbol. Ultimately, the status symbol of appearing rich publicly, while living poor privately is all a mask to insecurity. If you want to be rich, be yourself! Riches are worthless if you lose yourself in the pursuit of more. By being true to yourself, you now have something money can't buy, a peace of mind.

It's time to stop acting like a child at the checkout line with the candy everywhere. MINE! MINE! MINE! Not sure where our children could have possibly learned to go and buy anything that looks appealing to the eye. You might have to drive yourself a little crazy with brief sacrifice now to have inner peace and financial freedom later. Stuff is exactly what it says, STUFF. We get stuff to STUFF our life with things that rust and fade away. Stuff never satisfies completely. If it did, you wouldn't have to keep buying something new every few months. Too much time spent on upgrading the phone, not enough time spent on upgrading the bank account. Stuff is a coping mechanism that makes you believe it will bring you happiness. STUFF the stuff out of your life to make room for what actually matters. You don't need brighter jewelry and newer shoes; you need to know your worth will never come from your stuff.

Money Character

Where your money goes your heart will follow.
Mathew 6:21 (NIV)

Currency helps us to feel current. We become current with the times by being resourceful. The funds you are able to obtain can do hopeful healing, or scary scarring; depending on whose hand it's in. Money is similar to a drug. It gives you a sensation of being high. You can do things with money that you could have never done if you didn't have any. There is a stimulation and excitement that occurs when we have some, and a feeling of sorrow when we have none. Money can elevate you or cripple you. The same money that can lead a person to destruction and devastation can influence another person to rebuild a city and feed the hungry. It's unbelievable how an item can be used in such extreme opposites. No matter how much money you have or don't have, the condition of your character needs to be improved. However a person spends their money reveals what is in their heart. People buy what they love and for the people they love. Riches aren't exposed by the amount in your bank, but revealed by the amount of love in your heart. Your heart condition is the captain guiding your financial condition.

If you love to have nice things, that is where your money will go; if you love drugs, family, entertainment, cars, vacations, then that is where your heart and money will travel together. Your heart and money are not completely separated from each other. One can't go in one direction without the other. They give permission to each other to make choices. The choices we make with money are a direct result of what we think about and how we feel about something. Your mind, money, and heart all work together to guide your decision making. Make sure you don't start with money to guide your heart and mind, but allow your mind and heart to guide the direction of your money. When you follow love and logic your purpose grows, when you chase money, your happiness goes.

If a foolish broke person wins the lottery, guess what? They are now a foolish rich person. When having a significant amount of money, you still need to be responsible or it can ruin your life. When we are blinded by money, moral and values can become corrupt. Acquiring all the riches in the world can't cure the brokenness of the human spirit. Money isn't the solution to character defects. The character defects only become more visible when an abundance of money is possessed. Money is one of the greatest tests of character. More money will equal more tests.

The reason money can destroys lives is because instead of money being enjoyed, its being worshipped. When money priorities are shifted to the top, everyone else is at the bottom. It's a heart thing, never a money thing. When you love money, you will always be broke no matter how much you have. When you love people, you will always have more money than you need, because having loved ones is true riches and money is icing on the cake.

What If?

Let's suppose for a moment that everyone in the world was given 10 million dollars. We are assuming all things are equal and all people have equal opportunity. Let's fast forward 10 years from the day every person in the world was given 10 million dollars. How many of these people would be broke, and how many would have even more money? Can you imagine some of your friends and family members going broke in a few years? Can you imagine some of your other friends and family having more than 10 million $? I am sure you can. Everything would work itself out and we would return to the same scenario before everyone received their 10 million. The rich would be rich and the poor would be poor. Some people who had ten million dollars will end up in poverty. We all know that we can't control the families we are born into. Some people are born into wealthy families and others are born into poverty. You still have the choice on what to do with the family legacy. You can continue in the dysfunction or build upon the assets. There would be multi-millionaires as well as people living under bridges. People would become billionaires, while others literally penniless.

Money doesn't fix peoples priorities or their habits. People need to be fixed first, with self-control and discipline for money to have the proper impact. Those who were theoretically given 10 million dollars will spend what they believe will get them to their goal. If you had 10 million dollars where would you be in 10 years? Financial freedom is about what you do, with what you have. Where will you be in 10 years from now financially if you keep doing what you have been doing? Don't like what you just envisioned, then stop being childish with your money. The quicker you grow up, the faster your money will grow up and mature with you.

Freedom

If you live for the moment with money, you will find a future with an empty pocket. Piling debt isn't cool. Some people will have more money than others; we aren't all meant to be millionaires. Some will struggle more than others. The only person you should be in competition with is yourself, only you can change you, not anybody else. Everybody wants to be free, but won't stop committing the crime of unhealthy spending habits. For any freedom to exist there will have to be sacrifice of comfort. No dollar amount equals Freedom, because freedom isn't bought, but it is costly.

FINANCE DASH - PART II

"Beware of little expenses. A small leak will sink a great ship"

Benjamin Franklin

War

I can remember a time specifically when I was on a tour in Iraq. I didn't have to pay for food, gas, rent, electricity; I didn't have any bills at all. I thought to myself, "This is the life, all this extra money and no bills to pay." During my year in Iraq, I had a moment to reflect that still sticks with me to this day. I remember having more money in my life at that point than any other time. I had so much money I didn't even know what to do with it. As I stared at my paycheck in the blazing sun with a slight breeze, I thought I have never had pockets this full, with a heart this empty.

You see, I was rich with money but suffered with a broken heart. All the money with nobody to share it with, all the financial resources with no happiness; I was in poverty. I had reached my financial goals while losing my peace and purpose in the process. I achieved my desires, but failed to see my gifts. The gift of love became a stranger in my life. My only friend became money, and those dollars don't make the loneliness go away. The greatest war we face is not in a military battle, it is the relationship between our money and God. Too often money becomes our god leaving our spirit shattered with brokenness.

When I think back to that day, a breakthrough came because I realized you can have money and still be broke. Since that day I decided I am not going to pursue money to make a living, rather pursue my purpose and use the money to make a life worth living. What is money truly worth if we don't understand the value of life and our relationships? I received all the money I ever wanted and failed to get everything I needed: a relationship with God and a loving family. Start your financial plan today and don't live for the cash, live for priceless riches in your dash. No matter your spiritual beliefs, we typically spend a season of life making money our god. What you think about the most and spend the most time on will become your god. Money was my god and no matter how much I had it was never enough.

Abuse

If money brings happiness, celebrities wouldn't end up in rehab. The money can't fight the depression of your negative thoughts or provide comfort during worry and anxiety. Too often, we worry about people robbing us of our money. We either think of criminals, IRS or outrageous store prices. I can assure you; nobody has robbed you of more money than YOU. Your habits and choices rob yourself of your financial future. Money is more often abused than used. Money will buy things and very nice things, but can't make you a nice person or financially responsible. For your health concerns you find a doctor, who do you turn to for financial health concerns? Find someone who can help and turn your challenges into change. Make sure they are finance professionals (not lottery winners or broke people). Get help, the love of money is an addiction as well, and can cause health problems and relational conflict. If there were a rehab for being addicted to money, I am sure there wouldn't be enough rooms to fit everyone. The good news is that you can change. It's not too late to recover, when you have an ounce of hope you can produce a pound of change.

Get Schooled

From the time we can count to one, we should know how to count one cent and one dollar. We need to educate our children about mathematics in finances, rather than algebra (Sorry to the algebra teachers). We go to school to receive an education to prepare individuals for adulthood. We are told to be adults; much of being an adult is paying bills. Without any proper training on money management paying bills consistently, will become a consistent problem. We live in a system designed for people to financially struggle. However, school students can tell you all about calculus math problems as if that will pay the rent or feed their future children (sorry again to the calculus teachers).

The moment you can count, count some money and learn its value of being added and subtracted. The education of math with money will save you from future financial disaster. Learn about one of the greatest wonders of the world, compound interest. If you don't know what it is, google it right now! After you google compound interest, go and learn about how to make your money grow like grass by watering it with proper investment accounts.

With the American dream of getting a good job, owning a home, getting married and having 2.3 perfect children with the white picket fence. The dream sounds great, but the dream is costly. When dreams are costly and not carefully spent, the dreams become broke and so do we. Even having your dream job can't save you from the nightmare of mismanaging your money. Don't wait another day to educate yourself on something you use for the rest of your life.

Think

If we take the time to think to ourselves what the benefit of this purchase is, or will I use this in 5, 10, or 20 years from now, we would most likely decrease our spending habits. Many purchases are done on impulse because it has the bells and whistles. We have a short-term desire for a long-term problem. It isn't having more stuff that is the answer; it's being content with having less. Take time to reflect on the importance of each purchase and decipher the difference between a need and a want. Do you need that? Or do you want that? Asking this question is a sign of maturity, and then acting on your needs instead of your wants produces wisdom. When you have wise decision-making habits, you allow your money to grow old and wise with you. Think before you buy, there is a motto to live by.

Be the Change

If you want to change the world, start by giving some change away. Not only in change from something different, but the change you received back from that coffee this morning. A dollar doesn't exist without being made up of 100 cents. It makes sense to give cents, since others need it more than you, that's common sense. People cannot become poor by giving. Have you ever met a person who said I am broke because I donated money to help those in need? I doubt it, but I am willing to bet you have met someone who is broke from spending money on their wants. There is much confusion between genuine needs and lustful wants. Children buy what they want; adults invest in what they need. When we add financial resources to others, we multiply our own value and financial gain. When we subtract our money for ourselves, we divide our bank account in half as well as our hearts.

You and I have something in common. We both know about organizations where people all over the world who have way less than us, and we sit back and do nothing. It is devastating to learn that we all know people personally who are struggling financially, and we have refused to help them. It is our responsibility to step up and step out with a financial leap of faith to support those in need. With so much poverty and darkness in the world, we are called to use money as a light to guide the path for others. Every time you give, your heart grows more and so does your bank account.

Work Until You Die

Let's imagine you are planning to invest your time on living your dash instead of a trading all your time for a check. The person in our scenario is named Tom. Tom enjoyed his childhood and teenage years. The first 17 years Toms was growing up and going to school. Tom gets his first job at age 18 and retires when he is 68 years old. Tom hates his job but because the money is good, he stays working there. Tom has spent 50 years working and has spent the majority of his life collecting his check at a job. 50 years in the workforce is most of our lifetime because most people don't live to 100. Tom retires at age 68 and has 10-15 years to hopefully enjoy life. Unfortunately, at the age of 68, Tom's health isn't what it used to be. Now Tom is using the remaining years of his life trying to get his health back. Trying to stay healthy becomes a full-time job. Tom's plan was to be retired not *Be*-tired.

Those years in the middle are huge chunk of our lives. When you are growing up the first 18 years you are a child. The last 18 years of your life you are an adult child. Both spectrums require limited independence. Choose the prime years where you are truly a healthy adult to make responsible financial decisions. Do you really want to spend the majority of your life bored, frustrated, and not pursuing the purpose you were designed for?

Do you really want to work at a job spending dreaded hours watching the clock? Or do you want to be excited to invest your life into your purpose in a career where you're living your dash and living life to the fullest. You could spend 50 years of work hours, hating and being disgusted with life. The 5 decades of your work life should feel more like an investment of your time with passion instead of dread and boredom. The half century can be invested or wasted; you get to choose which one you will have.

You might be thinking while that's easy for you to stay, I have debt, children, student loans, car payments, credit card payments and I need to pay the bills now. Don't just randomly quit your job, be strategic and plan to pursue your purpose. If you're not sure what your purpose is, ask yourself these 4 questions for some assistance. 1) What am I good at? 2) What do I enjoy doing? 3) How can I help others with my idea? 4) Can I get paid for it? Take a moment and ponder your answers as it should give you some direction on where to go next. Now is the time to search until you find your calling. If your calling has you stressed or broke it's not your calling.

Ask Yourself

What is the one thing you could stop spending money on, and start investing money in? Who is the one person you should stop spending time with and who is a person you should invest your time with? What is the expense that truly matters that you can't cut from the budget? On the other hand, what is the one thing you constantly spend money on that is selfish? Asking yourself questions about how you budget your time and money will frequently remind you if you are on the road to freedom or stuck on the highway paying another toll. Investing your money and time wisely is fundamental. See how the word fundamental has the word Fund and Mental. The two are interconnected. A healthy mental state leads to healthy financial funds.

Spend or Invest Time

Imagine how it would sound for people to say, "I am choosing to invest my time today". Now before you get confused, allow a moment for me to expand on this idea. We have all either said or heard others who have said, "Ugh I have to work today," or "Man, I have to work," or "I don't want to go to work;" these are all typical complaints. Rather than saying, "I have to go to work," you could say, "I am going to invest my time today." Simply saying, "I am investing my time." makes us more aware of the importance of time. When we use our gifts that we have been given to invest our time while earning money in the process, our vocation is no longer a chore, it's an honor. Saying I *got* to go to work means something completely different from saying I **get** to go to work. If someone asks you what time do you have to work? You can respond, "I will be investing my time from 9am until 5pm". Even if you don't view it as investment you can trick your brain into believing the importance of cherishing the time.

Your purpose is where fun and work meet together. You can either be a prisoner to something you hate (job) or be a prisoner to your purpose (career). When you love your employment, you get two checks instead of one. One check is what you get financially, the other check is the joy gained from a productive investment of your time.

A Blast From The Past

Does anyone remember when they were young getting measured against a wall with a pen or pencil to see how tall they were? The line on the wall represented an accurate measurement of growth over time. I remember getting measured, and going back a few weeks later to see if I got any taller. The same principle can be applied to measuring our finances. What gets measured will reveal growth, or expose what we have neglected. When we get on a scale, we measure how much weight we have lost or gained. We measure our pay rate by the hour, salary, or commission. When you get taller, you are growing, and more is expected of you. When your money grows you will also have more that is expected of you. With more money, there are more choices, bringing more responsibility. Measure your money, not with anyone else but yourself. Grow up and grow your funds. You are no longer a little child needing others to measure your growth for you. You are designed to grow; only your unhealthy habits can limit your progress. Make one more financial decision today that will empower you for tomorrow.

Extra Tomato

Too many people think about the dollar amount on their check and not enough on where that dollar amount is going when it's cashed. Counting money without counting expenses is like ordering a Big Mac meal with a diet soda and saying, "I am eating healthy because it's a diet soda." We must consider the magnitude of the Big Mac. Every Big Mac or salad eaten brings either a negative or positive consequence. When making purchases, don't think just about the price, learn about the value.

I remember a time when a few of my friends decided they were going on a diet. The goal was simply, stay away from unhealthy food. We all went out to lunch in a location that had some healthy options and some unhealthy but delicious food. As we received our food, we met at the same table to eat together. My two friends who were on a diet ended up with two completely different meals. One meal was a salad, the other was Taco Bell. My one friend with the salad looked at the other dieting friend and said, "Why are you eating Taco Bell?" His response is something I will never forget. He said, "It's all good, because on one of my burritos I asked for extra tomato."

I wanted to slap him for his stupidity, but all I could do is laugh. Don't make a poor investment with your money and expect a great outcome. You can't participate in unhealthy habits and expect healthy results. Don't hope for the big lotto ticket to cover the cost of your foolish mistakes. Don't bank on striking it rich at the casino. Don't become an extra tomato guy.

Money Motto

Too often we think by exerting more effort, we will yield greater results. To further explain my idea, think about person number 1 running on a treadmill for 30 minutes. After they finish, they eat a Snickers bar. Compare that to person number 2 who only runs 15 minutes on a treadmill at the same exact speed. The difference is that this person eats a grilled chicken and salad after. You see the difference? More isn't always more; more is only more, if it is more effective. More time doing something and making more money does not equal mature responsible decisions. You could make 60,000 dollars a year and the guy next door with a similar financial situation earns 45,000 dollars and yet still has more money than you. That shouldn't be the case but often it is. It's important to have good effort and earn money, but it's even more important to learn what to do with what you earn.

The more you measure your finances, the more likely you will become disciplined in keeping it. Waste money and you essentially waste your time, which leads to wasting your life. Increased income doesn't mean decreased stress. Being thankful and knowing you are blessed will help you pass the finance test. Since one of the biggest stressors in life is money, it's time to jump on the scale and weigh your financial options. There are times to spend, save and give. You have a choice in which way you tip the scales of money. Get ready; your money is waiting for you to catch up to your potential. Once you have a good financial plan, your life plans will give you a secure future. Start your plan, follow the plan, and discover the power of the financial dash legacy.

Finance Dash Goals

Identify 2 people that can help you set and achieve specific financial goals within the next 30 days.

Identify 1 resource (websites, books, podcasts, which will provide you with financial education within the next 30 days.

1)_____

2)_____

3)_____

FORGIVENESS DASH -

"Forgiveness is not allowing someone else's faults to live in your heart."

Native American Proverb

Forgiveness is one of the most painful and rewarding processes to go through in life. The intentional reason forgiveness was placed in this book directly before the family is because family won't function properly without it. Forgiveness opens the floodgates for cleansing and washing away the pain. When we are left out, hurting, and struggling to heal, questions begin to run through our mind, questions such as "What did I do wrong? Did I deserve this? Why would they do that to me? Why can't I forgive them"? Ask the questions, seek the answers, and rid yourself from the terrible taste of bitterness. No matter the difficulty of the situation, everyone advances quicker when they discover freedom through forgiveness.

Forgiveness Effect

How we view our recovery process from the unfair events that have occurred, make the difference between being stuck in trauma or becoming resilient. The effect of forgiveness will cause people to know they were victims, but they won't remain victims. Forgiveness shifts perspectives from being a victim into being a survivor. Your dash will have pain, suffering, loss, abuse, addiction, and disaster in some way. This isn't meant to discourage you, but prepare you for unavoidable pain. The unfortunate reality is you will experience pain to the point that if you don't forgive, the pain will be even greater. Each challenging circumstance represents a necessary step you might not completely understand. As long as you still breathe, you will have battles. Fortunately, the battle is temporary, and the legacy of healing from forgiveness lives on forever.

To live your dash, you NEED to forgive. Not only forgive the small offenses but even the things you think are unforgiveable. There's freedom in surrendering to someone else's painful choices from continuing to reopen scars that almost healed. You should forgive, yes, but don't let people take advantage and allow repeated offenses if they are avoidable. When you permit certain behaviors without correction, you endorse the inappropriate actions. It's common to think of a time where we allowed people to walk all over us. Don't be a doormat but provide a welcome mat for those who threw dirt on you. Welcome them and thank them for the valuable life lessons their behaviors taught you. Then you can throw the mat away and recognize your worth more than being stepped on. The best way to show you haven't been defeated is to give kindness and forgiveness, even when it's undeserved. When you do that, a ripple effect of kindness through forgiveness, touches the soul of everyone you encounter.

Offended

We are so quick to be offended and then be defensive. For forgiveness to exist there must be an offense to begin with. If you are constantly offended, then you better be constantly forgiving. That doesn't mean you never get offended, so you never have to forgive. However, it does mean in this extremely short life, it is important to choose your battles wisely. Most people don't even know they offended you, but you are still demanding restitution for something they are unaware of. You desire an apology, while they are unaware of your feelings. Choose to forgive whether they know they hurt you or not. If you have an opportunity to address the offense then do so, if not, you still should forgive for the sake of your sanity.

Some things will take years and decades to forgive, but the sooner you forgive the offense, the less time those negative feelings fester in the atmosphere. Forgiveness is not a spectator sport; it will require a call to action which needs to begin with you, not the perpetrator. The offender may never know or care how much they hurt you. On the other hand, you know and it's your responsibility to not allow other people's negative choices ruin your life.

The harder it is to offend you, the more secure you are. The easier it is to offend you the less secure you are. When you have chosen to live for your legacy instead of other's opinions, you have gained an abundance of security in your identity. If you overflow with forgiveness, you bring a drought to insecurity. When you know you are valuable no matter what any person says about you, there will be more room for forgiveness and less space for stress.

Hurt and Heard

The more people are hurt, the more they need to be heard. We strive for people to understand and accept us but refuse to share our hurts with them. Being brave enough to welcome your wounds and talk about them encourages and empowers others to share theirs. When we share in the open what hurt us in private, we gain back a piece of our confidence that we once lost. When you share your story, you turn your hurts into healing and your wounds into your wins. Sometimes the greatest hope you can give another person is to share your experiences when you were hopeless.

We all have a story and your story is powerful. Nobody in the world can tell it the way you can. The painful screams of the past soon become whispers. What was a whisper of pain soon turns into silence. Pain isn't only meant to wound; it's meant to teach. When the struggles are shared it demonstrates how all our stories are connected. Once we realize our stories are connected, we add the power of the forgiveness dash to the next chapter in someone else's character. Vulnerability is rare. By being open and honest about our pain, we invite others to grow through suffering with us.

When we suffer together, we become bonded for life. We know what it feels like to be emotionally deceased, and with a kind word or a patient ear, we can be renewed. There is that voice inside of us that wants to scream out what happened to us, but we hold back for fear of being judged and rejected. We desire a certain image to be maintained. Truthfully, letting someone close enough to really know the real us is the most frightening of all. Having the mask of perfection only hides your true identity. We are all scared warriors looking for someone who will love us just the way we are. Let your hurts be heard, so you can silence the pain and flourish in growth together.

PROtect

When you were rejected and neglected, understand forgiveness is the way to be protected. Forgiveness delivers protection from letting the trauma dictate your future. Forgiving is one of the hardest things on the planet to do. We struggle to forgive, because something or someone robbed us of justice. Something or someone was taken without our permission, and payback seems to be the logical approach to getting back at the world. To access new life means letting go of strife. Some pain, you never truly get over, but you can get through it. Allow yourself to grieve and discover hope so you can cope. Through all hurts there is healing if we desire to get well. When you are ready to release the burdens that are trying to bury your potential, you no longer are trapped by the pain, but released from it. The hurt sometimes is too painful to fully heal on earth; however, you can make strides daily to recover. Letting go will empower you to throw away the despair that impaired you, giving you strength to be repaired. Witness the afflictions you once carried sink into the sea of bitterness as you rise from the depths of defeat and rise to redemption.

Blame

"We tend to be very good lawyers when it comes to our own mistakes but very good judges when it comes to the mistakes of others."

David Zastrow

Whether right, wrong, or in between, blame gets shifted from one person to the next. Where blame lives, forgiveness becomes forgotten. You can still hold others accountable for their actions while relieving yourself from the exhaustion of holding onto their poor choices for a lifetime. To forgive and forget is simple to say but rarely in action. As long as blame remains, forgiveness cannot develop. Spending a lifetime pointing your finger, will point you in the wrong direction. Blaming isn't always necessarily wrong when someone needs to be held accountable. On the other hand, we need to be ready to accept when someone else's finger is pointed in our direction. When you blame, you remain the same. Blame is a strategy to express concern to change a circumstance, instead of a changed mind and heart. Many times, our pain is valid, but when we hold grudges for too long, our condemnation of others becomes a coping skill to refuse changing. Even if you can't change the awful actions of another, you can change your attitude about what happened.

Doctor

Without forgiveness we inherit a bleeding wound infecting our hurts on others, while searching for a doctor in all the wrong places. You won't find a doctor to heal you with a bottle, drug, sex or gambling. We all have quick fix doctors that we hope will cure us, not realizing they provide nothing life lasting. It's like eating food; yes breakfast, but breakfast isn't enough. We wouldn't dare believe breakfast in the morning feeds our hunger at night. We don't think breakfast will hold us over for 3 days, weeks or years. It's foolish. The doctor of forgiveness needs to be pursued daily, multiple times like eating a meal. The fun and damaging habits daily won't fill you up; it only prolongs the healing process because you were prescribed the wrong medicine. The cure isn't in a prescription, if it were you would be recommended to swallow the pill of pride. Pride prevents most of the freedom forgiveness provides. Once you remove pride you add endless possibilities of growth.

Go Heal

Naturally, people lean towards problems instead of the solutions. Acknowledge the pain, for only what is acknowledged can be changed. Once you have identified the hurt you need to pursue what will help you heal. Accept that you have been hurt and realize your worth. You are NOT what happened to you; you are what happens inside of you. Only when you have spoken up about your hurt, will you have the opportunity for others to come along side of you and nurture your wounds. When you have a small cut, you only need minimal support. A Band-Aid or some type of ointment will help. For the deeper more serious wounds more attention is needed. The deeper the emotional wounds the more friends, family, counselors, pastors, and mentors you will need. Never be ashamed of your hurts, be proud of them. Our scars are meant to help deliver other people from theirs.

Understanding

The more we understand the human condition of being flawed, the likelier we will give forgiveness to others. We give more freely to some based on the platform we have given them in our lives. When we place other people on a pedestal and they let us down, the hurt we have received is much more damaging. When we come to understand that people will let us down, disappoint and hurt us, we become accepting of the possibility we will need to forgive people in advance. A huge challenge is expecting other people to act, think, behave, and believe the same way we do. When others live in opposition or differently than we do, we think there is something wrong with them.

We fail to realize that something is possibly wrong with us. Or maybe neither of you is wrong, you are just different. You can disagree with someone and still respect them. Try it sometime. I promise you won't die from it. From the government, to sports, families, friendships, employment, all avenues and relationships bring differences. Either the differences make you indifferent or make the difference in success. This causes the belief we are always right; leading us to believe we are superior. Once you begin to think you are better than someone, you treat everyone worse. Understanding people were specifically created to be different from you is designed to strengthen humanity, not divide society. We would much rather defend and react rather than listen, understand and respond. Find the common ground even if the common ground is that we are consistently different. We are all in the same boat, even when we are rowing in different directions.

Freedom

Forgiveness is not weakness or letting the other person win. Its empowering yourself to not let other's actions control your emotions and behavior. Forgiveness is a true sign of maturity and strength. It's a purposeful decision that declares to the world, yes, you hurt me bad, but my desire to heal was stronger than your desire to hurt me. Go ahead and declare that the one who intended to afflict you was supposed to bury you in pain; however, you dug yourself out of the pit. Their dangerous actions were meant to restrict your life, but by being resilient you discover freedom from captivity. My guess is that you have some pain you still are holding onto. You want to let go. We all desire letting go, but we haven't figured out how to open our fist yet.

Look at You

"And why worry about a speck in your friend's eye when you have a log in your own?"

Matthew 7:3 (NLT)

If we can truthfully and humbly admit that we are our own biggest challenge, freedom will arrive much faster. We put other's flaws under a microscope and place ours in a telescope. Before you can blame, judge, or criticize others, you must first address some of your own issues. This doesn't mean we dismiss those people. It does however; cause you to hold yourself accountable to your own thinking, actions and behavior. Boundaries aren't barriers to relationships, they are bridges. Could it be we have some conflict in our relationships because we have subconsciously allowed or permitted the fear of confrontation to rule? If you have the strength, confront the offender. If not, confront your heart about why the uninvited guest has been allowed to remain a part of your identity. It's better to pick up the mess in your yard after a little bit of wind storm than a hurricane.

The longer we draw attention to the addict, thief, lazy, poor, rude, racist individuals; we forget about one extremely important thing......... OUR OWN FLAWS! The longer we throw dirt on someone, the harder it will be for them to get clean. We aren't called to shame and blame. We are designed to take people's messes and teach them how to use their hopeless mess, to create a hopeful message. When people are out making bad choices, it's important to recognize that they are still working on their story. Assess your own life before you ever judge someone else's. The hero in them hasn't been discovered and they are still searching. Some of us are detectives and find what and who we are looking for at a younger age, while others take their time in a game of hide and seek.

The longer you look at someone's flaws and magnify their setbacks, the less time you have to work on the real problem, which is YOU! The media can trick you and make you believe that it's the government, education, religion, and every person in the world who has an issue, except for you. If you are reading this and thinking you are a good person and it's really all the other "bad" people, then you are deceived. When you are deceived, you usually don't know it. That's why it's called being deceived. If the entire world can shift blame onto others, we would never assume that anything was wrong with us. Blame wants circumstantial change, without personally changing. When that happens, everyone accuses and tries to change others. The greatest change that needs to happen at any given moment is not another person or circumstance. The first and most important change will always begin with you. You can't hope for the world to change without first changing yourself. The biggest project on earth is not world peace, but inner peace. If we started with inner peace, then the world would follow.

FORGIVENESS DASH - PART II

Imagine

Can you imagine carrying bitterness to the last day you have on earth? I can't, and I don't want to. Do yourself a favor and forgive your parents, yourself and those who have hurt you. There will be a new sense of purpose and you will be replenished with peace in your life. Even those who haven't learned that lesson yet should be forgiven because without it, you will suffer. A life without forgiveness is like waking up every day gasping for air because someone is still stepping on your oxygen tank hose. I am not saying forgiving is easy to do, but it makes breathing a whole lot easier.

Smelly

Not forgiving is a one-way ticket to spending a long time angry in a short life span. Forgiveness is cool. Not forgiving will get you in boiling hot water. It's literally disgusting to walk around all day and know someone else has your happiness. Unforgiveness reeks! It follows you around everywhere like a shadow. It becomes a part of you like a bad toupee. That fake smile can't hide the disgusting growth following you around. People can smell you as soon as you enter the room. It's like stepping in dog do-do. Sure, it happened yesterday, but every time you put those shoes on you smell awful and it follows you everywhere. Your presence is no longer enjoyable. Then, the heavy burden you have been carrying is subconsciously handed off to everyone else so they can suffer with you. Do yourself and everyone else a favor. Stop stinking up the place and start forgiving someone. If you can't forgive someone forgive yourself. If you want to stop stinking up the place, make a place in your heart for forgiveness and soon you will smell like fresh flowers.

Individuals making poor choices don't necessarily mean they are evil or bad, they have an unmet need. Stealing, lying, addiction, abuse, and other bad habits are not the real problem. Those actions are symptoms of a much bigger problem. Their negative public and private choices are reflections of their inward and personal lack of forgiveness.

Look past the person's actions, and learn why they act a certain way; and discover who hurt them and help them to forgive. Or help yourself and forgive. Forgiveness isn't only about words; it's backed up with behavior change. Talk is cheap, go and pay the price with some action to back it up. Before you take the time to walk someone else through that, you need to forgive everyone, EVERYONE no exceptions. Once you can do that, nothing can stop you. We all have trauma and pain to deal with. Unforgiveness has stopped more people than any crisis ever has. The greatest tragedy that happens in our life is not the actual tragedy, but the inability to heal from the tragedy.

It Will Come Back

The same amount of mercy you give to those who have hurt you will be returned to you in full measure. This statement means if you forgive people graciously, you too will also be forgiven graciously. When you love more, you forgive more, and when you have been forgiven deeply you forgive others deeply. The other end of the spectrum is also true. If you are stingy with your forgiveness, God and others will not forgive you as easily. Forgiveness comes back around full circle. The more forgiveness you give to the world the less the world can hurt you.

Don't become trapped and get in a cycle of allowing pain to infect your life. The boundary of being personally committed and in charge of your own attitude is freeing to the soul. We all desire to be forgiven. We think others forgiving us is a requirement; while forgiving others is optional. When we don't forgive; we must live with the consequence of not excusing others for their humanity. We struggle to overlook the mistakes of others as if we have never made any. Human beings are flawed and by design we all do foolish things that hurt ourselves and others. Go ahead and forgive. If you let forgiveness reside in your heart you will have peace in your mind.

Different

Failure can't exist with forgiveness. Even if you don't get the goal, being able to forgive makes success worth the effort. The temporary failure is not losing its learning. Think back to when you were a child and you broke a rule and got caught. I imagine you were forgiven for the wrong you did. If you weren't, I will assure you that you are forgiven by God no matter what you have done. All you need to do is ask for forgiveness and it will be given. Some of us are still waiting to be forgiven. In return we withhold our forgiveness to others. You can search for that forgiveness from people and never receive it. They might have moved on from the situation where you are still stuck on how they hurt you. Think back to another time you hurt someone and know you didn't deserve to be forgiven but someone was gracious enough to still forgive you. How did it feel? It feels great doesn't it? Break the chain of your pain, and release the trap of troubles, and discover the release of rebirth through forgiveness.

Time

The longer we wait to forgive, the stronger the pain takes a hold of our being. It becomes more difficult to GIVE when we believe nobody ever gave us the forgiveness we long for. We struggle to give what we have never been given from people. It's time to make a decision; you can continue to make the cycle or break the cycle. Declare in this moment that you accept that you have been accepted just the way you are. You are forgiven by God as soon as you ask for it. Say this out loud, "God forgive me for my mistakes, and I will live differently, knowing I have been forgiven". Although, it's possible no person has forgiven you and you haven't forgiven yourself, there is nothing you can do to stop God from forgiving you. Everyone is forgivable, lovable, changeable and acceptable through the love of Jesus. All you need to do is accept His love and forgiveness. You're not waiting on God; God is waiting on you!

Changed

No matter how many times we have been hurt God says we still have great worth. Forgiveness is the difference between regret and growth. Our dash would be crushed if nobody ever decided to forgive. Surrendering to God means that the pain that held us back now pushes us forward. The tragedy that trapped us, now allows us to triumph. Giving everything to God means we don't have to go to battle alone. God will fight with us and prepare us for every war we will face; where victory awaits. No matter how big the problem to us, God is bigger. No matter how long the pain has lasted, God's forgiveness, love and support lasts longer. No matter how deep the wound was, God's the great physician and His healing is deeper. All of this is yours once you accept his forgiveness. Without forgiveness it's a one-way ticket to suffering without a cure. With forgiveness you receive a roundtrip vacation of a lifetime to your favorite destination with all expenses paid for.

Give

The word forgiveness has a key word in it, it's called GIVE. The idea of forgiveness is to GIVE. The definition of the word give is *to freely transfer the possession of something to someone.* The actions of someone else pass along to us guilt, anger, shame, humiliation, unworthiness and the list goes on. When you don't think, feel or believe that you can give forgiveness, do it anyway. Always taking, takes you backwards, while giving moves you forward. Give without an agenda and give even when others are not worthy. Forgiveness has to be given. You don't forgive because they deserve it; you do it because YOU deserve it. Your success reflects how many times you are able to keep forgiving undeserving people.

If you can't let something go, then it will stay with you, wherever you go The feelings that come from not forgiving can sometimes be more devastating than the actual traumatic event. Feelings can't be minimized until they are transferred to God. Give it to God and let Him handle the worries. When you hand over those terrible things, you can possess something greater. To reach any level of greatness you need to release bad things and even good things to capture great things. You can't live in unforgiveness while hoping to have peace, joy, patience, value, success, significance, and purpose. Those concepts are in opposition to each other.

Lack of forgiveness ensures an abundance of extra weight to shoulder. If you have ever carried something before and then set it down, you know how good it feels. Your back, knees and joints have the pressure and tension on them removed. This is a simple image of how forgiveness works. When you hand over the luggage to God you can carry on with the journey God has designed for you. When you transfer the weight, you can breathe again and gain freedom to move towards significance. As soon as you lay down your burden, you have open hands to hold blessings.

Choosing to not forgive is choosing to cut open your wounds right when they were about to heal. It's not the event that consumes your life; it's your choice to not grieve properly that consumes you. When forgiveness happens you are empowered to move forward.

Giving is the greatest gift. Think of the greatest gift someone has given you on Christmas or your birthday? Or imagine the greatest gift anyone could ever give you, is waiting for you under the Christmas tree. Now imagine you never opened the gift. You heard about the greatest gift ever but for some reason you were scared. You were scared because you weren't exactly sure how it worked. You were nervous because you felt undeserving and could never repay the individual who gave you the great gift. You are hesitant because by accepting the gift, you have acknowledged all your needs haven't been met.

You see the greatest gift in the world is worthless if it's never opened and accepted. As soon as you open and accept the gift, everything is different. Your life will change forever, because your dreams come true. A debt you couldn't pay, a relationship you couldn't fix, a problem you couldn't solve, inner turmoil that wouldn't go away, and a loss that has sent you in a downward spiral; suddenly, there's hope. The gift of Jesus Christ forgiveness is waiting to be accepted by you. Jesus doesn't disqualify you because you have been hurt or if you have hurt others. Jesus wants your heart. He has already forgiven you. You just need to acknowledge the forgiveness. I challenge you to open the greatest gift ever given. The love of Jesus, who forgives all who think they are unforgiveable.

Forgiveness Dash Goals

Identify 1 thing you truly need to forgive yourself for doing no matter how long ago it happened within the next 30 days.

Identify 2 people you need to forgive whether they deserve it or not and completely forgive them within the next 30 days.

1)_____

2)_____

3)_____

FAMILY DASH -

"We spend most of our lives either trying to live up to our father's expectations or try to make up for their mistakes".

Barrack Obama

What I have discovered is, if you want a quality life you will need to have quality relationships. This topic of family is quite sensitive. For the remainder of the other F's, we have more options for that particular part of our dash. However, the choice of family is limited. We don't pick our parents, siblings, aunts, uncles, cousins, grandparents, nieces and nephews. It's quite difficult to separate the story of your life from the branches in your family tree. Family may not always be what we hoped or dreamed it would be. Ultimately, if it wasn't for them, who would you be? For some, challenges of family have been an obstacle, for others it has brought great motivation.

Not all family members are created equal. No matter how close the blood line relation is some family members you will love more than others. Some family has always been there for you, while others neglected or abused the relationship, they had with you. No matter what, we all have a family. Even as an orphan, an adopted foster child, a widow or divorced, we have family somewhere. Family life is complicated, but with the right attitude it can still be restored. Despite any dysfunctions, no family is too far gone to be being reunited and closely bonded.

Team

Even with limited family member choices, you still have a choice as to which direction your team is going. Your family is a team. A family is constantly either moving toward their goals or away from them (Whether there is a specific goal set or not). This team is like an army that has an unannounced ranking system of rules and order. The general who might be a grandparent, a parent who is a colonel, an aunt or uncle who is a captain, an older sibling who is sergeant and the younger generation could be a specialist. All have different roles, but all are valuable. Challenges arise when certain people become demoted for their lack of leadership, while some of the younger family members rise through the ranks quickly. Because certain family members believe their way is the only way and everyone else is wrong, tension is heavy, weighing down some of the relationships.

Just because you are the youngest in your family doesn't mean you are the least educated, or qualified to be a positive role model and example to your elders. On the other hand, being an elder doesn't mean you know best. All branches in the family tree have specific strengths, or limitations which can either hold the family back or push them forward. By not allowing other people's gifts to shine in the family, you essentially cut off a growing healthy branch. Allow everyone to shine and be watered to grow properly. In the family dash, there is constant movement. Through cooperation and communicating a vision, the family will go places they never anticipated. If no one is stepping up to the plate to hit a grand-slam-of-an-idea that will bring everyone home, then you need to be the one who is willing to take a swing, even if you strike out. It's better to strike out with strong effort, then to get out with lack of effort.

Father

For years in my profession there seems to be one common denominator as to why a family self-destructs, and that is the lack of a loving father. The father has significant impact on the entire family right from the beginning. If he bailed, and wasn't involved, or if he is actively committed, every decision of a father is passed down to his children. The decision that is passed down will either keep the children down or elevate them. Decisions you make today, even subconsciously reflect back to the relationship you had or didn't have with your father. We strive to be just like dad or nothing like him at all. If the father you were given was a bad example, use his life as a road map of what not to do. If the father you were blessed with was an excellent example, then take the time to build upon the great foundation that has been established. Either way, Dad has generational influences on the entire family. Choose which example you will follow. We need to rebuild through reconstruction of our hearts.

How you view your relationship with your father, directly impacts your current relationships. The way you treat your spouse, children, siblings and other family members is rooted in the way your father treated you. As a father myself, I have seen how my relationships have been affected by my own father. I'm sure my children will do the same as they continue to grow up. Fatherhood is a huge responsibility. As fathers, we all need to do better. We have more influence than we will ever know. If the role of fatherhood improves, the entire world could be different. I have yet to meet a person suffering with a significant amount of addiction, crime, personality disorders, poverty, to state that they have always had a strong, loving, trust worthy relationship with their father. The trauma that has happened to people during their youth has kept them emotionally and mentally like a youth. Although, daddy has a huge influence we still need to do our part. We need to learn where their reactive trauma ends and where our ability to respond begins.

Complicated

In the obstacles of family life, there are hidden and unspoken wounds that have not been addressed. Family becomes a spider web of inadequate coping skills leading to prolonged pain. The great thing about your hurts is that you can be healed. You don't always have to get along with your family and you don't even have to like them, but you should always love them. Don't love the hurt they might have caused you, embrace the lesson from the scars. Where there are wounds, there are overcomers. You are no longer a victim but a survivor. There is power in your family story; power to be resilient and break any cycles that have caused you harm. Family branches go in different directions; you have the choice to choose which way yours will grow. Although, some branches are damaged, all limbs can teach you something.

Memory

Naturally our brains are wired to think about the negative memories that have formed us. If we dare to be different and intentionally choose good memories to reflect on, we will heal a little faster. For some memories of game nights with board games, family dinners, sports, vacations, graduations, and just sitting around the house as a family can be a good memory. The challenging part is when the negative memories outweigh the positive ones. Hold on to the moments that gave you joy; made you smile and laugh.

There will be specific memories we have that were extremely important to us, that other family members have completely forgotten about. Sometimes the most memorable moments of your child hood your parents won't remember. You never know when one of your greatest memories will happen, or when your child's greatest memory will occur. When I bring up moments that were important to me my parents are unaware of what I'm talking about. The reason for that is my precious memories were viewed through a different lens than my parents.

Now that I have my own children, I can witness how this has played out in my life once again. Recently, I read a story that my daughter wrote in her class, which was explaining some of the highlights of her life. In her story she shared a time when her and her dad (awesome guy I heard so much about) went parasailing in the Bahamas'. I remember thinking, "Wow! That was one of the greatest experiences of my life!" I will never forget that day with her. It was our first time parasailing and it was special. The very next line in her story describing some of her greatest childhood memories mentioned playing catch with dad for softball season in the yard. I thought WOW! I was shocked. Playing catch really wasn't a big deal to me. But I learned it had a tremendous impact in my daughter's life. From that moment, I have a much deeper appreciation for the small things in life, because typically the small things are never small things. I never would have guessed something we did so commonly was so impactful. Apparently, I missed its significance until I saw it on paper, a year later. You never know when you can make your next amazing memory. As a family; appreciate any time spent together, because it can make a lifelong impact that passes on to your grandchildren.

Anthem

There will be certain memories that remind you of special family moments that you can't explain to others. There are probably songs, movies, or shows that take you right back to your childhood, and ones your children will never forget; ones they will sing and show to their children. If you could choose a song, movie, or show that represents your family, which would it be? Identify a theme song that symbolizes the identity you have as a family. While some family theme songs represent the current season the family is in, others may last several lifetimes. It's never too late to find a new family anthem that will bond the family together.

Create a family theme song and sing it loud in the car together. The simple moments of singing in the car together to a song that means so much to you and your family, will never be forgotten. Know your spouse, children, parents, and siblings' songs and learn to listen to the lyrics. Listening to their favorite songs will help you understand and bond with them on a deeper level. The simple idea of learning their favorite song, even if you hate it, will give you clarity into who they are as a person. Utilize music as a resource to draw closer to your family no matter the difference or taste in music styles. The difference in style is what provides the uniqueness of family. As each family discovers the family theme song; each individual still has their own song to sing.

Create

There are countless ways to connect with family members. Sometimes it will take creativity. Doing something you are afraid of doing with your family might be the exact thing your family needs. Taking the time to do something with your family that you don't even like, can be a huge challenge to the family unit. It's through the unknown that you come to know yourself. By knowing more about yourself you can reflect on who you are. As you discover the unknown together, you will educate each other more about your likes and dislikes. Taking risks can breathe new life and energy into your family. When you face your fears as a family, you are courageously bonded forever. When you step into the unfamiliar, you grow in familiarity of your loved ones.

Try This or Don't

Are you familiar with the term trust fall? If not, you can watch videos on YouTube. I tried this exercise with my young daughters. I did not fall and crush them either FYI. I had them come up to me and perform the trust fall. We planned ours, as a trust building activity. At first, they were extremely hesitant to fall backwards without seeing if they would be caught. There were several times where they were terrified, and they wouldn't do it, until one of them got the courage to try it. After witnessing that I was trustworthy, my other daughter became brave and did the trust fall towards me. With each time I caught them their trust in me developed. Not only were we building trust, we were building fun memories together. I can tell them to do a trust fall anywhere and they will do it without hesitation.

One time I gave my wife a heart attack because I was having them attempt some extreme trust falls. I had them climb a tree and fall straight back from several feet high off the ground. This is usually the difference between moms and dads; dads are a bit more extreme. My daughters would drop from high heights and I would catch them. They would laugh with wonder and excitement. They also conquered their fear of heights by knowing dad would catch them. Each time they tested my trust our relationship strengthened. You don't necessarily need to do trust falls to build trust. You can simply keep a promise; do what you say you will do, or any other practical idea. The point is, something as simple as doing a trust fall, strengthens the bond in the family. When trust is extended the relationship is secured.

Mentor

Are you familiar with the term marriage mentors? My suspicion is that the idea is new to you. If people understood that the quality of marriage shapes our entire society, we would take marriage and marriage mentoring much more seriously. When a marriage is struggling, a family is hurting; when a family is hurting, a community is harmed; when a community is harmed our society suffers; when society suffers, humanity becomes confused and settles for second best. We all should be learning from others and since marriage is the beginning and the glue of the family unit, then finding marriage mentors should be a high priority. The rhythm of the marriage dictates what song the rest of the world will sing, whether good or bad. Seeking out married couples who have been married longer and have a stronger marriage is essential to a thriving marriage.

When we were children, hopefully we had parents that taught us how to become adults and what marriage is supposed to look like. If we didn't, we still have the opportunity to seek out someone who can be our marriage mentor. A mentor for your marriage doesn't simply improve your marriage, it changes your work environment, your mental and physical health, the success of your children, and even your crazy annoying neighbors can be positively influenced. Great marriages don't happen by accident and inspiring families don't happen by mistake. There needs to be consistent, intentional interactions with others who can lead us in our marriages. Without guidance in your marriage, life after I **do**, will feel more like I **don't**. Once you realize that the entire world is impacted by how you manage your marriage, you will take it more seriously.

Battle

Some family members are central to peace while others insist on war. We need to be peacemakers instead of peacekeepers. A peacemaker communicates the problem and presents a solution, explains feelings and forgives with a plan to move on. Peacekeepers try to keep the peace, but are people pleasers who hurt their families with silence. They don't want to rock the boat or make waves, and are scared to offend anyone because they might not be liked. They want everyone to be happy and no real peace actually happens. A peacekeeper wages a silent war in their mind, while a peace maker has loud chatter ending with a hug of reconciliation. Families have both; you are one of these two in your family.

This confrontation is done out of love for the well-being of the family unit and needs to happen for progress to occur. I have been a peacekeeper and am working on becoming a peacemaker. I know that when I strive towards being a peacemaker, I uncover the wounds and bandage them with healing love and forgiveness. No dash is problem free. Through solving the problem, the dash experiences freedom when a healthy solution is communicated.

In each family you have a role to play. Some are considered the black sheep while the other is the favorite. One family member might be the one who is the glue and holds the family together, while another might try to tear it apart. No matter the role, all are important. We can't look down on certain family members who suffer from addiction and are untrustworthy, because even the most difficult person on the planet has something to teach you. If all of my family members were like me, it would be a disaster. Even if you are the most educated and successful person in your family, remember to humble yourself. Everyone is ignorant in some subject. Know that all roles are equally important and need to be appreciated. The uniqueness of each family member provides a special dynamic that only they can provide. Know your role and respect the roles of others. Encourage each individual in their specific place. When roles are identified, they strengthen the family causing a strong structure of support.

FAMILY DASH – PART II

"A happy family is but an earlier heaven"
George Bernard Shaw

Giants

Every family will face a Goliath at some point; a monstrous giant challenge that appears invincible. The bigger the giant, the harder they will fall. The harder they fall, the stronger the family grows together. It's not during the times of prosperity that family is strengthened, but during times of vulnerability. For every problem, there's an opportunity for family development. When the big problem has developed, an even bigger solution is needed. Families become bonded for life if they don't let the grief divide them. The giants are scary and uncomfortable, but without them we become too comfortable being mediocre and take for granted the love this life has given us. When one giant falls, another rises, and through those trials is when family, becomes a family. Be a giant slayer and celebrate the victory together. No giant problem is greater than the solution of love and family.

Deeply Rooted

Have you ever wondered what your family name means? If not, take the time to research more about your family history. Having an understanding of your family roots will help you become more resilient in overcoming adversity. You will understand what helped your family roots develop in the past and learn how to plant some of your own for the future. The historical influence of your parent's names and their parents' names provides a rich family education. When we are oblivious to where we came from, it's much more challenging to know where we are going. You have an opportunity to carry on the dash legacies that preceded your existence. You can carry on the name or change your family tree by taking a different lane to the dash highway. Make the decision to continue family tradition or blaze a new trail. You decide how your family will be remembered based on the choices you make today. Leave a legacy that is worth talking about with your grandchildren at the dinner table.

Reflection of Family

As each day passes, we are one day closer to the end of our lives. We need to take the time to reflect on how we have managed our family relationships. We leave a legacy of hope or hopelessness behind to our loved ones. Take a moment and think deeply on the legacy you are leaving behind if this was your last day on earth. If you feel uneasy, regretful, or worried, this indicates it's time to make a change and transform your legacy one decision at a time. Make your family proud and give them a family name they are proud to share with the world. No matter the family relationship you have, you will be influenced, and you will be influencers, intentionally or unintentionally. Family isn't strictly holiday's and birthdays, where you get together to reduce the guilt of not seeing one another and doing your annual duty. Don't play your role out of duty, but out of love. Choosing to love people when they are unlovable is one of the most loving things you can do.

Planted

The family tree is literally your roots and heritage, the stump is what binds you all together. No matter how long and different our branches become, we are still connected. Some branches fall, rot out and become unhealthy and are removed from the tree. Some others grow fruit and flourish to expand the tree. Some branches break while others bend. Family members might plant other trees. Be careful what your plant, for what you plant is what you will get. How you plant your family is how your family will grow. If a family's foundation is growing on lies, anger, worry, anxiety, depression you can't expect fruit to grow. The fruit will rot, and the tree will wither. If you plant your family tree on love, respect, kindness, faith, commitment and provide enough sun and water, fruit will grow, and the family will reap the benefits. Some families have a shaky foundation, but you don't have to build your life with a similar blueprint. When you are old and wise enough to plant your own family, choose not to repeat compounding mistakes from your family's history. You are only one decision away from planting and building your family on a better foundation. So, the question is, what are you waiting for?

Mission

Finish this statement. The most important priority in my family is _____. The answer guides the direction your family is currently taking. Take a moment to ask each family member for their answer and see what people believe is number one. Family members may each have a different number one. Depending on their answer, if they say love is number one, ask them how they demonstrate love to others. If their answer is respect, ask them how they demonstrate and want to be respected. Knowing what your loved one loves, helps the family to feel unified as ONE family. Start speaking each other's love language, and communication will transform your family for life.

Estranged

Because of certain circumstances families drift apart. As you lose touch with those you love, you lose touch with a piece of your identity. By thinking you are being the better person by always separating yourself from the negativity, you need to truly assess if it's the right thing to do. By removing this person, is it because you are mad at them and can't get over it, or is there something truly happening that will destroy your life by associating with them? In this fast paced society, we go from a strong bond of family, to estranged strangers in danger of never rebuilding a broken relationship. A connection was lost, damaging all parties involved and they both have their own story and they are sticking to it. Sometimes it's the circumstances that you were raised in that have a huge impact on the negativity you have today. Some attitudes and lifestyles become inherited. You don't get to choose the family who brought you up, but you do get to choose which family you allow yourself to stay in. Take the good and add to it and take the bad and remove it. Doing this, takes years to understand, but if you can do it, go at it with 100 % intensity. There should never be a time of blame for how your life turned out based on your parents and family members. You do get to choose what is added and what is edited from your life story.

Connected

Connections are very important, when you lose a connection on your phone its common to be frustrated and inpatient. My guess is when you lose a connection with a family member you don't freak out as much as you did when the call was dropped, and Wi-Fi isn't working. As soon as you lose service on the phone you make another attempt to complete the task you were just performing. There is no hesitation because you desire connection instinctively. Why don't we instinctively crave family connection over Wi-Fi connection? I think the Wi-Fi connection is an easy distraction from the difficult family connection, so we gravitate towards what's easy, rather than what's important.

Once the connection in your family fades away you don't move in a direction to establish the connection again; you travel far away to a dead zone with no service and no chance of a connection. How much more important is a human connection with family, then a connection on your cell phone? We all know it's not even comparable. It's scary to have uncomfortable conversation with those you love. Consequently, it is those difficult conversations that hold the family together and reconcile relationships. I am not recommending you get into any drama; I am urging you to give family another chance. We have all fallen short and have made countless mistakes. Let your family just be family, which is a code word for an imperfect human being. Remove your unreachable expectations and have no expectations, other than to love one another. You can work out all the other details later. I dare you to move out of the dead zone of isolation. Search for a connection between those you have lost contact with, no matter the reason. We become as strong as the connections we are born into, the ones we break, make and rebuild. Go out and rebuild what was once destroyed, and turn the disconnection into the right direction through reconnection.

Something To Do

Think of something you do alone on your own free time that you could include another family member in to participate with you. Inclusion provides solutions to small family problems because the relationship has common ground to walk on. What is something you could teach another family member and what is something a family member can teach you? Even your children can teach you something. It will take sacrifice to teach something new to someone, and a good test of patience provides an answer key to your interactions with one another. When you do some-THING together you become some-ONE to your loved one.

Obsession

"We should never place our happiness in anything that could leave our lives"

C.S. Lewis

As important as family can be, they actually can become too important. Hard to believe but it's true. Family is everything but it's not the only thing. This isn't an attempt to persuade you in thinking family isn't important. That couldn't be further from the truth. What I believe is that we can become obsessed with our family members. Our spouse, children, parents, siblings and in-laws take on a role they were never meant to have. We place too much of our happiness on others, especially family and it's not right. If something or someone you love could get up and walk out of your life or could be lost in some other way, it should never be number one in your life. If that person leaves or passes away, they essentially take your happiness with them. By placing your happiness in other people and things, you have a life that is not stable in this ever-changing world. People are not responsible for our happiness. Your family members love you and you love them, but let's not worship and idolize them. We have turned our loved ones into our worshiped ones. We have turned them from human beings into our god. We idolize our children and spouses to the point of it being unhealthy. We should love them with everything we have, but they won't provide ultimate peace and joy. There is only one family member that won't ever leave, and that is God.

Since we do place family at a high priority in our lives, when the expectation is not met, it can even be more tragic. The agony of pain and hurt when they disappoint us is too much to bear at times. The closer the relationship, the deeper the wound when they decide to hurt us. It's quite difficult to put people and things in their proper place. We either don't display our love for our family enough, or we obsess over them much. None of what I am saying is to discourage a loving relationship, but more about having inner peace. To have inner peace is to be content even without things and people that might not be there tomorrow. This is a hard pill to swallow. Your ability to love your family is one of life's greatest gifts. It should never be neglected or overused. Now is the time to love appropriately in the boundaries of your dash. There will come a time when you pass away, and they will pass away. The question is are you prepared, and are they prepared for the next life that awaits?

Related

People believe family is who we are related to through blood, marriage and adoption. Family goes way beyond that. Family is also the ones who love and respect you no matter what. They have seen you at your worst and are still around. They have your back with no questions asked. The people you can't ever imagine your life without have been adopted into your heart and you have inherited family. It is those who are connected to your heart, rather than your DNA that indicate who your family is. A bloodline of love inside of your heart is more powerful than a shared last name and similar physical features.

Family will appear in different forms. New family members might come disguised as a friend, co-worker, neighbor, church member, or from other walks of life. Being related is exactly what the word itself indicates, the ability to relate. When you can relate with others, and they with you, a new birth of family members is born. This happens because of the unity of relating with one another. Look beyond biology of relationship and discover interpersonal relationships.

If you have pursued your family dash, you have been blessed with blood family and relational adopted individuals who transform to family. With so many flavors of family we can acquire family in multiple avenues. There is work family, sports family, spiritual family, family-family, friend- family and so on. When you incorporate family members from diverse backgrounds your family tree expands and strengthens. This will empower you to bounce back when setbacks attack.

I want to focus on the spiritual family for a moment. Being spiritually connected provides you with a spiritual family. The spirit and soul have united and now are related. The spiritual bond is a bond nobody can ever take away. In a spiritual family there exists a group of people who hold the same beliefs, values, and morals. This family is encouraging and supportive in your journey. The spiritual family becomes a part of the bigger picture, a holistic approach to your lifespan through a purposeful dash and life in eternity. The film of the bigger picture is where you go when your dash runs out. People can point you towards God or away from God. You either will listen to what the world tells you or be led where the spiritual family is leading you. Decide who you will allow to affect your dash and your final destination.

Spiritual families serve a common purpose, to love God and love people, when people do those two things, the entire world changes. Since everyone is designed for family and God created family, no one can teach you more about family than God. God wants you to be a part of His family even if you have been hurt, addicted, abused, neglected, divorced, gay or atheist, it doesn't matter. God still wants you to accept that you have been accepted just the way you are. God's family is meant to guide you to God's plan which is greater than any human plan. The greatest form of love is unconditional love, and nobody gives unconditional love like our Father God. In my experiences, the better my relationship with God the better spouse and parent I become.

Family Dash Goals

Identify 2 people in your family you will be more intentional about developing a healthy relationship with over the next 30 days.

Identify 1 person in your family you will limit spending time with over the next 30 days.

1)_____

2)_____

3)_____

FAITH DASH -

"My brothers and sisters, what good is it if people claim they have faith but don't act like it? Can that kind of faith save them?"

James 2:14 (NIRV)

Making the decision to pursue all these F's in your dash will cause you to miss the mark for your life if the most important F is not present. For it is without faith you can do nothing. It is through faith that all the other F's depend. The less faith you have, the more you worry and become frustrated. When everything and everyone else fails, faith is the supernatural choice to change everything.

Some people aren't in agreement with the concept of faith but will go to work with faith in getting a paycheck. Unfortunately, we place faith in things, people, and circumstances then wonder why we aren't fulfilled. We go to sleep at night and have faith in tomorrow, or turn on our cars and have faith they will start. Whether you realize it or not you do have faith! This is small faith, but a little faith is all you need. Small faith precedes big faith. If you can have big faith in small things, imagine how much better it would be to place small faith in a Big God. No matter your faith, it will be tested. Only God stands the test of time, all other people and things will pass away.

Faith Will Rise

Most of us are familiar with the term leap of faith. It's when people do crazy things we only dream of and wish about. Daredevils, adrenaline junkies, or people who are bold enough for public speaking are viewed in some ways as brave. This extreme approach doesn't make people great. It's that they have great faith. Those with great faith will do great things. There are two constant choices we are making daily. One is to either to live by what is unseen (faith) or live by what is seen (world). More faith is more trust; which is less doubt and less worry. Faith will need to be activated blindly. We won't see or know what will happen, but at the same time, have an overwhelming comfort and peace in knowing something greater is in store for us. This leap will require you to live beyond your own human understanding. Take a moment, and recognize there is Someone greater than you, greater than the human mind can comprehend. When you jump and leap not knowing Who will catch you, it is in those moments we are rescued by our faith in God. Now is the time to jump into the unknown to bring you closer to the one who knows you best. Faith will rise when your comfort zone drops.

Pond or River Faith

Faith is not something that is stagnant like a pond; it is a river that continuously flows and moves in action. For example, if I say, "I have faith that when I retire, I am going to have 3 million dollars ." That's something I believe with faith that will happen. I need to believe I can get the three million dollars before I can see the three million dollars. Faith believes first, and see's second. In order for faith to come alive, we need to be like a river and put our faith into action. If I haven't saved a penny, but expect 3 million dollars in retirement, I have become what I call the pond mentality- one with no action or effort to live your dash and think faith will do it all for me. Faith without any action is not faith, it's a wish list. God is not a genie who when you whine and complain you get your needs met. Prayer with no deed is equivalent to the lazy man who wonders why he is in poverty.

A river can produce energy because its movement, a pond doesn't produce productivity. When you make the decision to switch from pond faith to river faith you will make wise decisions. Pond faith is the basics of going to church, praying, reading the bible. River faith is putting those concepts into action. Pond faith is Sunday, river faith is Monday through Sunday, it's not an event, and it's a lifestyle. It's wise to put your faith in river action. Faith keeps you afloat when you're sinking in sorrow. God provides a lifejacket, so you never drown in complacency. Decide today you want a flowing river of faith in God instead of idle faith in people and things.

Don't Scare Them Away

We don't have control over others; however, we should be in charge of our own responses. I am willing to bet that at some point in your life people of "faith" have scared and scarred you, turning you off from the idea of faith. People have failed you and appeared to be hypocritical and judgmental. Perhaps that someone has been you at some point in your life. I personally spent several years refusing to have a relationship with God because some "Christians" were not a good example.

There's where we go wrong, we look to people for answers instead of God. We become too dependent on pursuing the invention, not the inventor. Countless flawed people will disappoint you. Even your greatest role model, mentor, leader, spouse and everyone on earth can and will let you down at some point. We are called to something greater, not everyone will respond to the call of God. Sometimes people respond to God's call responded inappropriately. Your parents might have caused you to run away from God forever. At some point though, you need to grow up and stop blaming your parents, pastors, or other so-called Christians for your lack of faith. God isn't going to ask you at the end of your life about the faith of anyone else - except yours. So why do we spend so much time dwelling on poor examples? Let the poor examples teach you a wealth of wisdom. Their walk with God, whether good or bad can show you what to do or what to avoid. You can stereotype an entire belief system based on a few people's inability to live their beliefs responsibly. This causes people to lose faith or refuse to even have any to begin with. Don't let someone's poor and selfish example ruin God's amazing plan for your life. We should never let the flaws of people turn us off from the perfectness of God.

Unseen Faith

Faith will produce questions such as "how can we really know that God exists, if we can't see God"? Faith is comparable to the wind. We can't see the wind; we don't need to see the wind to know its power. We can feel the winds impact in our lives and those around us. Wind changes the environment and the stronger the wind the more impact it makes. The wind is invisible, but we believe in the wind. We believe in the wind because we feel it on our body, and we see the effect of it. Faith is no different. We don't see faith; however, we witness the impact. We feel it in our body and see lives and communities changed because of faith. Faith, similar to the wind, will blow you away, refresh, and surprise you when you feel its power. How much greater would your life be if you dared to believe in something greater? The power of faith is stronger than any tornado winds. The creator of the wind moves in a similar fashion. He wants your attention without being seen. Next time you feel the wind recognize how symbolic the breeze is. Let every breeze be a reminder to unseen power working in our lives.

Cell

My pastor shared this concept of faith with me years ago. We don't know all the ins and outs of how a cell phone works. We have a general idea, but most people don't have a 100% understanding. We have faith when we send a message or make a phone call, it will communicate to the person we need to communicate with. That's one small example; there are countless. The oxygen we breathe is not something we really need to think about. We don't have to wonder if our lungs are going to work, we just breathe and have faith that when we breathe, we will continue to live. We know some basics about how we breathe but most of us are not doctors. Yet we still have the assurance that when we take a breath we can breathe, (that's faith) small faith, but it's still faith. We don't know all the functions of everyday things that we do, but we continue to do them with faith that they will work despite the fact we don't know how they work. These things still work even when we are clueless to how they work. Faith is similar in regard to that. We have an idea of how it works, through prayer, worship, commitment, and other biblical principles. At the same time, we aren't going to know how faith works 100% of the time, and that's perfectly fine. If God needed us to know everything, we wouldn't need Him in the first place. Accepting that you won't ever know all the answers is the first step towards growing in wisdom and faith. If God wanted you to have all the answers, you would be God, but you're not. You just don't know, and that's alright. However, you need to know the One who does.

Pass Away

We all pass away physically but that doesn't mean we all have to pass away spiritually. The same barriers that once held you a captive prisoner, can be the same motivation to set free. The chains of misguided pleasures, and old thinking habits now shatter before your eyes. You are no longer in over your head drowning in regret, but now are breathing with a reserve tank of oxygen. That new breath gives you air you couldn't breathe before. God is a God of second chances. Be cautious because you never know if you will be alive for your next second chance. Knowing that we expire should not scare you but inspire you to greatness, and all greatness begins with faith.

Worry

Worry begins when faith ends. The trembling fear of the unknown paralyzes your ability to follow God's plan. You become captured by uncertainty and riddled with anxiety. Even if God told you specifically every day of your life you would still find something to worry about. Either way, you feel scared because you fear what you know, and you certainly fear what you don't know. Faith is not in what you know; it is in who you know. The more you know God, the greater the opportunity for you to sleep with peace at night and wake up with purpose in the morning. We all desire answers, but those answers aren't found within yourself, or others.

Verdict

In a courtroom, when deciding if someone is found guilty or innocent, the jury comes to a verdict. There is a conclusion drawn from the verdict. Once the decision is made, the outcome doesn't just change because we feel differently from when the decision was first made. Our faith is on trial and we need to come up with a verdict. The great thing about putting your faith on trial is that it's never too late to be found not guilty. You have a loving Savior who says we are innocent despite our guilty past, present, and future. When you make the decision to believe God and in God, your faith will be tested. Tests can be tiring but not losing faith will refresh you for the next test. Just because life is unfair or difficult doesn't mean God doesn't exist or isn't powerful or loving. God is waiting on you to make a decision. The decision to believe in God regardless of how you feel; beliefs are not your feelings. Make the decision to go from being guilty to being innocent. This happens by giving your poor judgment to the righteous judge who has righted your wrongs.

God will judge you and people will judge you, but it is only God who can take his perfect judgment to an imperfect person and still love, forgive and accept them. From his acceptance and your decision to follow the faith you have placed on trial; you can be finally free at home with Him. Test the faith. Push it to the limit and allow an all just, powerful, and loving God to turn your sense of guilt and doubt into innocence, faith, and redemption.

Dream vs. Nightmare

Frequently, people are inspired by their dreams or paralyzed by their nightmares. When you have faith, you will be moved to act on your dash. Faith enhances clarity of the dream God has placed in your heart. Dreams and nightmares can happen at any time. The greatest dreams and nightmares occur when you are awake, not sleeping.

Fright and night often go together because the dark is scary. The worst dreams are called frightmares. Frightmares are what you fear, and then you act on those fears. They are the fears that surface because you lost sight of the dream. A dream is keeping the faith despite not having all the answers. We will either run towards our dream in confidence, or run from our nightmares in terror. Unfortunately, most people allow the fear from their worst nightmares become a real-life living theme. When your belief in the dream of your dash outweighs the fear of the nightmare, you can successfully step into your calling. Faith propels you to pursue something that will outlive you.

You don't have to be sleeping in order to be awakened to opportunities that are surrounding you. When your faith in God is stronger than your fear of success or failure, you develop strength to battle any setback. There are billions of dashes that were crushed by not following the dream. A dream is within all of us, and the dream becomes real when your faith does. Dreams turn to reality, and happen because of faith. Nightmares can occur from an absence of faith. Incorporating faith doesn't need to happen during the "perfect circumstances" since perfect circumstances don't exist. The perfect time to utilize faith is during imperfect circumstances. Since we live in an imperfect world, it's always the right time to activate your faith. No matter how scary life gets, God will protect and provide for you when you call on Him. Not always immediately, but on God's time. Your dreams can still come true. All it takes is a little faith in a big God. Your faith dash has seasons of sunshine and storms. When you have made the conscious decision that no matter what you will believe and follow God, all those nightmares aren't so scary.

Battle

Faith has the power, so that during your biggest battle you can still have peace. It is the peace to know no matter the result, we know the one who has the final say. When we reach out to God and scream, He patiently listens and whispers back restoring us, those tough battles become smaller when God becomes bigger. The problems shrink as he is magnified. You will be battle tested, and through your faith God will fight with you, and for you while keeping harm from you. And if any harm does come your way; the healing process is always better with God than without God. While on earth the absence of pain is not promised. In fact, when you live long enough one of the promises you will encounter is that suffering, and pain will be a part of your story. All the battles you face on earth no matter how tragic, will be something you forget about when you have achieved victory in heaven.

Storm

When the storms of life come raging at you unexpectedly, we often wonder, "Where is some shelter to protect me"? Faith is the buffer that prevents you from drowning during the storm, and gives you water during the drought. The umbrella doesn't appear to make as much sense to have during a sunny day. It becomes almost a necessity when a storm hits. Faith seems to make more sense when storms around and within us are happening; losing a loved one, a financial crisis, natural disaster, or broken relationships are all examples of storms.

During times of crisis it makes sense to have that umbrella of faith to protect, and keep you safe and provide comfort. The umbrella works best during a storm because it is during crisis that we know we are not in control and need something else to give us the support we desperately long for. The umbrella isn't only for the storm it's also on a day where everything is going well, and the sun is shining, Umbrellas can also be used during the sunny, beautiful days. If the sun shines too much we get burned, too much of anything can cause damage. Too many good days can somehow cause us to think life is good because we are something spectacular. No matter weather, an umbrella of faith is still necessary. Be thankful for the storms because without them you might have never sought God and discovered your purpose.

Circumstantial

Faith is not circumstantial. Many circumstances will influence your decisions, but they don't have to be the ultimate deciding factor. It is not circumstances that should change your faith, but faith that changes you to improve your circumstances. When bad things like war, terrorism, starving children, and school shootings are happening people begin to question God. When bad things happen, God's existence comes into question. What people fail to recognize is that God is not circumstantial. Just because something bad happened does not mean that God doesn't exist or care. In fact, it is through the chaos that God's mercy is magnified the most, the healing and restoration that takes place after tragedy is God working through trials.

People wonder how this can be God's will. All these terrible things, and life isn't fair, still doesn't change the love and power of God. God has a will, and so do people. The Devil also has a will. Because God doesn't force and freely gives, things happen that don't align with His plan. I don't agree with the terrible things that happen, and if you have questions for God and are mad at Him, it's okay. You have the right to feel that way. Life isn't fair, and God never said that it would be. Typically; during the challenging times of this world people keep blaming God. Or ask how could a loving God allow this to happen? That's an excellent question that isn't always answered on this side of eternity. One thing for certain is that we all do have free will, many times that free will is abused. Sometimes, it's for people to step up and share God's love and lead other people to Christ. Other times it's that God's love will be shared, and Gods healing can be revealed as stronger than any worldly wounds. I have learned it's alright to not know everything. That is why faith is so important. Faith says I don't know why this is happening, but I still trust you God. It doesn't make sense, but I know we will get through it.

FAITH DASH - PART II

"Your faith can move mountains and your doubt can create them"
Anonymous

"And we know that God causes everything to work together for the good of those who love God and are called according to his purpose for them."

Romans 8:28 NLT

If you have ever baked a cake you know that the individual ingredients are disgusting. Raw eggs, sugar, salt, butter and many other ingredients are needed to make a cake. None of these things would we eat by the spoonful. When isolating ingredients individually it's a disaster leaving a terrible taste in our mouths. The same is true when we isolate individual events in our lives. We only see things as they appear currently. We don't think about how the tragedy and setback will become something greater in the future. No cake starts out delicious. Anything great will have some terrible things included. It is through the terrible things terrific things are born. When everything is all said and done and all things are mixed properly together, the reward is greater than we ever imagined.

With so much suffering, it's easy to question the concept of God. Since God is a Loving Father and we are his children He knows more than we will ever know. When people ask, why an all-loving God would allow all the suffering of children all over the world to exist, I think they have an excellent point. I would have to answer this question in different terms to help people understand.

I am a parent. I think all parents know (or they should know) that when we bring children into the world all parents are aware that their children will have struggles. Some of our children will have sicknesses, cancer, have their heart broken by a girlfriend or boyfriend, face depression, low self-esteem, become a victim of a serious crime, have friends stab them in the back, people will make fun of them, struggle financially, not make the sports team, drop out of school, get beat up, be suspended from school, get bullied, die at a young age. All these things are terrible. No loving parent wants these things to happen to their children. But when parents are realistic, they know that some of these things will happen. I know as a father my children will experience a variety of these tragedies. Some of them will be very unfair and my children have done nothing to deserve them, yet they might still happen.

As a father I choose to bring children into the world knowing they will face tragedy, pain, and suffering. Does that make me a bad father? No, I don't think so. Should I have chosen to not create children because the world is unfair? Should I have avoided having my children being born because I know that someday they will be hurt in ways that I don't like? If I could go back in time and prevent them from being born so they don't suffer or face trauma, I would never change it. I will love my children despite how bad life gets. This doesn't mean I am not loving, or caring. I could have chosen to never have children because they might suffer in a broken world. They could get cancer, be bullied, go to prison etc., but all that didn't stop me from creating them. I eventually decided that would be even more selfish to not let them live because I didn't want them to have any struggles. With every struggle they have, I hurt as well. There are some tough challenges I could prevent; however I can't attach a bubble to them permanently. When they start walking, they will fall down, and it will hurt. I still have to let them take their own path.

The same is true with God. He has allowed his children to be hurt the same way parents have allowed their children to be hurt. It's not that I want my children to be hurt, but I do know that pain is a necessary ingredient to life. I don't love my children any less than anyone else. God doesn't love his children any less because some suffer more than others. In fact, when my children are hurting the most is when they most feel my love. It's when they suffer that I can demonstrate how much I love them. God will show everyone who wants his love how much He loves them if they accept his love.

One thing I find quite interesting when people question God is that they leave out some of the world's current events. This frustrates me because people become so caught in speculation that they forget the blessings that have happened. During the chaos if God does exist, he must not really care. This is also not true. If the idea of God not existing because bad things happen in this world, then the opposite must also be true. If bad things happen then God isn't real, if good things happen then God is real. The idea when you break it down is ridiculous. For those who think bad things equal bad God or no God, you would also have to admit that good things equal good God. God is not circumstantial and lives beyond them all. God is so big and powerful and beyond what our small brains can comprehend that you won't ever figure it out. Even google gives out inaccurate and misleading information. It's alright, to not know it all. God exists whether you had the best day or worst day of your life today. No circumstance can change God because God created all things. Today is the day to make a decision and declare I chose faith no matter what, because God loves you no matter what has happened to you.

Transform the Dash

Let's suppose a person born in 1950, died in 2015. Their dash would look something like this, 1950-2015. Depending on their decision to believe in the creator, their end would not be in 2015. Their beginning would be in 2015. How encouraging is it to know that your loved one's dash has no expiration date? You won't look at their grave and be as discouraged because their time ran out. Instead, you know their time is just beginning. The dash no longer represents their first breath to their last breath. It symbolizes a legacy of faith that extends past your time on earth. Even living to a 110 is nothing but a breath in comparison to heaven. The longest living human being is not even a fraction of what awaits those who choose to live forever in heaven with God through faith. Even the longest life is a vapor of mist disappearing from earth. The world goes on, but do you?

Vertical Horizontal

Relationships have different dynamics but ultimately, they fall into two separate categories. The horizontal relationships you have with people and the vertical relationship with God through faith. When we pursue and put our horizontal relationships first, our priorities are not in order. When our vertical relationship is pursued first, we have the wisdom and discipline to understand our horizontal relationships more clearly.

This is the formula. Vertical relationship first, horizontal relationships second. The stronger the vertical the stronger the horizontal. Since God, (the vertical) knows what we need; He is the best option for guiding you to lead others towards what they need. When you desire to improve human relationships, don't look to humans, look to God. Since God designed all relationships, you will better understand the importance of both relationships.

In all my experiences when I have put my vertical first, my personal relationships have become stronger. I personally became a better husband, father, son, friend, and worker because I prayed and sought God for guidance. The closer we come to God the closer we grow with others. If you place your horizontal human relationships as your god and place God second, chaos will erupt more frequently. When you honor God above all, God will elevate your influence and love with others. Before you stare horizontally, gaze vertically.

Crossroad

Numerous times in your existence you will have an intersection where faith and doubt meet. You will have a decision to make, either follow your doubts our trust in God. We are all on a journey traveling down the road of life trying to find our way. Even on the 6 lane highway where all the other doubters are traveling at extremely high speeds, God will provide an exit lane of faith for you to take a break and refuel with his love. When you reach the crossroads, you need to choose faith before your doubt causes you to run out of gas. Refuel with faith. That's what gets you through the dash on the highway. When you're drowning in problems, it is by faith that God will provide a life raft.

Garden

A garden is an excellent representation of what occurs in your daily life. There's going to be dirt, predators, storms, and sunshine. A garden can't just magically withstand the elements that come against it. The garden must be closely watched and evaluated. Putting up a boundary or fence from potential predators that could try to destroy all your growth can leave you starving. It's not all about the fence in keeping certain people away; it's also about protecting yourself from what might try to devour your progress. The fruits of your character need to be protected. The protection isn't designed to trap you, but free you from harm. The safety risks are being minimized not to diminish your freedom, but to maximize your potential to grow. When you initiate your faith, God protects you from predators whose main focus is to reap the benefits of your resilience. Don't ever allow the enemy to take what God has given you. By gaining security through God, no storm or drought will stop the fruit of your character from developing.

Wrestle

"If I'm wrong about God then I have wasted my life, if you are wrong about God you have wasted eternity"

Lecrae

Many people think, "Well I have doubts; therefore my faith must not be strong". I would say just the opposite. The more you wrestle with God the deeper you are seeking to know Him. Ask the difficult questions and discover even more challenging answers. For great faith to exist there has to be a time where great doubt existed. After you have wrestled and still don't know, ask yourself "what do I have to lose"? For those of you who don't believe God exists, or if you are right about no God or after-life; then when you die you will live in darkness and nothingness. By being correct about your assumption, you have still ended up in hopelessness. However, if I am right, then we all have the opportunity to live in heaven in light, love, and peace. Which sounds more appealing?

This sounds like a no brainer. I am going to take my chances on God over nothing every time. I would rather risk heaven being real with 1% probability, than 99% certainty of no afterlife. Better to live my life pursuing a God that doesn't exist and finding out he isn't real, then to live my life as if God doesn't exist and discover He does.

Commitment

Although faith can be a one-time decision to believe in God, it is a continuous commitment. Your faith in God is what empowers you to be in his presence. All relationships grow when all parties are committed. He remains committed in all things and doesn't waste an ounce of your tears or pain. Rather, He will mold and shape you into the greatest version of yourself. Every tragedy brings triumph eventually. No matter how inconsistent our commitments to God are, his commitments are always consistent to us.

Talent

If the talent you have in life is singing, cooking, athletics, fixing, teaching, giving, just know whatever it is, you have a gift. The best way to grow your gift is to reflect the Giver of all gifts. Since all gifts come from God, it is wise to ask Him what your gifts are. Ask Him how you can best use them. Because of the gift; we gain confidence, even if you don't always live up to your own expectations or the expectations of others. To have faith you will need to have confidence. To be confident you will have to trust what your eyes can't see. Recognizing no matter how much you know, there are countless things you don't. You might not even know your own gifts. That's why relying on God will provide you with the opportunity to share with the world what God has blessed you with. Trust that God gave you the gift and talent to represent his grace and goodness in your life. The gift you have is designed to encourage and inspire those who are hurting. When you have crossed the line and declared that you will live your life for God you will be given even more gifts. You will gain what is called spiritual gifts. There are several spiritual gift tests you can take online to know your spiritual gift. God gives and gives more when you give up being your own god. Spiritual gifts are a promise and when you accept Christ as number one in your life your spiritual gifts will be revealed to you. No matter the gift, even if you think it's insignificant, it's a present to someone.

Bed

At any moment your death bed can arrive. Don't wait with hopeful expectation that you will get to grow old on that death bed. This is exactly why the decision to choose faith in Jesus Christ is of the upmost importance. Later doesn't always come. If later doesn't come, will you be 100% certain in knowing where you are going when you take your last breath? Even if you are at 99.99 % certainty, then there's an ounce of hesitation in your answer; which is a pound of guilt you carry. Release the hurts and guilt from what has held you back from being ready to die at any moment. Begin the process of knowing where you are going. Each heartbeat and breath we take daily is one more second closer to your closure. The clock is ticking, and the alarm clock of life always goes off before you are ready to wake up. When you stay ready, you will be ready when your time has come.

Struggle

The struggle is beautiful, because struggle produces strength. With any dream or goal coming to pass strength will be required. Frequently, in life, the greater the struggle the greater the reward if you don't give up. Welcome those struggles because they are a requirement to redemption. If you aren't struggling in life you are doing nothing of value or not being challenged enough. For it is through the struggle you will rise above what once held you back. The more frustrating the struggle, the greater and more purposeful the calling. If you think to yourself that you have many struggles, just know you have many victories approaching.

Just Be

For a moment think about eternity, and where you are going when your last breath arrives, taking time each day to just *be*, instead of just *do*. We have a constant need to do something but not to just be still. To "do" helps you feel like you accomplished something. To be gives you a moment to recognize who has already accomplished the greatest task. The task of sacrificial love has been done by the Creator. The choice to accept his love and think about how you can grow close to him is the most important task you can ever accomplish. Next time during the hustle and bustle of the fast-paced life that has you stressed, take a second and reflect, and know you have been blessed.

Hold On

Have you ever tried to hold water in your hand? It doesn't really work. Water can be carried in a cup or bottle and other utensils but surely not in your hand. You can attempt to hold onto the right things but without the support, it won't work. When holding onto things you weren't meant to carry alone, without the proper equipment, (like the water) opportunity slips through your fingers. Quit trying to hold on things you were never meant to carry. When you carry the right thing with the wrong tools, you go in the wrong direction. When you are going in the wrong direction, your ability to achieve your goal becomes weakened. Pursuing the easy route will stop you from reaching the challenging first place you have been striving for. If you get to first place with ease, consider the fact that the first place you achieved wasn't the end goal you were designed for. Although one of the biggest crime's humans commit is settling for second best; that shouldn't be the goal. If you gave your best and reached second best than you should be proud. It's better to have a challenging second place, than an easy gold medal.

Your God

Truthfully, we all have a god. Even an atheist has a god. A god is something or someone in our hearts and minds we place above everything else. It has our time, money, heart, attention, and thoughts. For some it is the love of money, sex, drugs, career, and yes even your spouse and children can become your god. Whatever you prioritize as number one in your life is your God. You can have several gods' that feel good and give you excitement and yet still be so far from the purpose of your dash. The wrong god can't take you on the right path; however, the right God guides you on the correct path even when things have gone wrong. The all-knowing, loving and just God, loves you and has sent his only son Jesus to save you from yourself. He is looking for a relationship with you. If we choose to receive his love, the greatest relationship ever created can begin. Whether you believe God or not, He loves and accepts you just the way you are. He wants to give you a blessed life on earth and in eternity. All you need to do is say accept His love.

Thinking back to those other gods you might have; what have they done for you? What will they do for you and will they be with you after you move on? Search and seek and allow yourself to be found. God is calling out to you. You will hear Him when you slow down long enough to listen.

Limitless

The ground you stand on determines how and where you walk. A firm foundation will provide a path for you to walk on even if the path is difficult. There is a promise to reach the final destination no matter how difficult the terrain. Faith in others and your own ability turns opportunities into obstacles. Faith in God's power transforms your limitations into prosperous positions. One of the greatest ways to stand with pride is to kneel in humility. Let God be God, not your definition of who you think He should be.

The less faith you have, the more limitations you place on yourself and others. In your own humanity, things are impossible. But with God all things become possible. The more faith you have the less restrictions will hold you back from your potential. Faith frees the boundaries that have trapped you in a box of what you can only conceive in your brain. Increased faith expands your strength to do something which was previously unthinkable. Things go from grief into goodness, hurt into healing, and the lost to a desired destination. Faith is the distance from impossible to improbable, then from possible to probable eventually reaching a supernatural reality. Small faith in a huge God is completely limitless. Remove the limits set by you and others by allowing a limitless God to love you unconditionally no matter your past.

Tombstone

You have an expiration date to your dash. At some point the number will appear on the right side of your dash. The choice to accept Jesus Christ as your Lord and Savior will dictate what happens after the dash. You can choose heaven, or you can choose hell. None of your great deeds guarantees you heaven nor do any of your destructive decisions guarantee you hell. You are only saved by the grace of God. When you accept Him you are able to receive this precious gift. You can do nothing to convince God to start loving you, and you can do nothing to stop God from loving you. To be welcomed into eternity with our loved ones and God we will have to make some decisions. First, we accept that we have sinned (missed the target for our life). Next, accept that Jesus died on the cross for your sins and mistakes and He is the son of God, then you ask for forgiveness, and ask him into your heart. Now you are a part of God's forever family. You now have the greatest gift ever given, eternal life; which is being given to you when you chose to believe. You have the chance not of a lifetime, but infinity lifetimes.

Every mistake, failure, addiction, abuse, divorce, loss and pain won't trap you anymore. He makes all things new. He is the wind that gives you the fresh air when you can't breathe. The breeze that refreshes your soul and gives you the peace you have spent your entire life pursuing. You are only one decision away from receiving the Greatest Gift ever given, and it all begins with faith. Accept that you have been accepted, and allow faith to awaken your soul. For without God your dash is terminated on your last day on earth. With God your dash is fulfilled on earth and perfected in heaven forever. Nothing is greater than unconditional love from an unconditional Father providing you with never ending life in heaven.

Faith Dash Goals

Identify 1 mature Christian you can ask questions to about Faith.

Identify 1 Church and Christian support group in your community that you will attend within the next 30 days.

Identify a specific time throughout your day to read the bible and pray for at least 5 minutes for the next 30 days.

1)_____

2)_____

3)_____

Conclusion

The 8 F's in your dash all possess a significant role in your life, and when one piece is missing, the puzzle to life is not complete. Each F will strengthen the other, empowering life on earth and beyond. Some F's are strong and continue to grow while others are still developing. We don't need to become overwhelmed and think that we have several F's we need to change and fix today. We are all under construction and not a finished product. No F has reached its potential. Start with one F that you have been disregarding and make the decision that life will be lived one F at a time, one day at a time, which will equal one dash for all time. Soon you will be able to excel in each F each day. There will be setbacks and speed bumps, but the things that slow you down are only meant to give you a cautious yellow light, not a forever red light. A green light happens, not always when we want it to, but when God says we are ready.

You are a witness to every person you meet. You are an inspiration for others to live their dash. The dash formulates a huge impact for generations. Your life isn't only a life. Your life impacts countless people you might never meet. If tomorrow never comes, will you know that today was pursued with purpose? It's time to dash to your dash and attack the future presently and be free. Create the dash you were designed for and know it can't be done alone.

I don't like to think of the inevitable dash that we all encounter as some kind of an end; it is more of a beginning. Although, all decisions are critical to a life of purpose, the compounding small choices lead to life-changing huge decisions. Before making big life decisions, decisions such as having children, getting married, changing careers, going back to school, buying a home, moving, religious beliefs, etc., take some time and go for a walk. Take a walk through a cemetery. Take a look at all the tombstones and read the names. Look at any other symbols or meanings or words that are on their tombstone. Think about them as people. Ponder the dates they have breathed life on earth. By taking a moment to see their dash, it brings a sobering reminder that we are not invincible. All decisions need to be made with wisdom and a clear conscience that today's choice is the next generation's consequence. All F's will be passed down and inherited eventually. The choices in how you develop the F's in your dash don't solely remain in that specific F. All the F's are connected and bleed into one another, expanding the influence of your story into someone else's.

Knowing that any moment we can be called into the afterlife should cause us to live intentionally and purposefully. It's important to ask if my last breath comes today; can I live with this decision? If you are making a decision that you are comfortable with, you will have peace about the decision affecting your dash. If you pass today, will this decision benefit your family, friends, and society? If not, change your choice, and give yourself a voice; a voice of change and influence to improve the quality of your legacy and empower others to discover transformation and freedom.

The performance we show to others is the exhausting façade we display to the world in hopes they might applaud our efforts. We grow tired, seeking a thank you that might never come. The mad dash in life will have people who never take the time to thank you for the difference you have made. People will disappoint and hurt you, as you give your final performance and last breath on your final day. When your time draws near to move on, it won't matter what anyone said about you. For where you are going, the opinions of people won't matter anymore. Since opinions don't ultimately matter for your eternal future, then they shouldn't matter in your temporary life on earth. As tiring as it can be to display flawlessness to the public, it is more exhausting to believe you can maintain wearing a mask of trickery. We all wear masks in certain relationships and situations. We too often hide our true identity because we don't accept or think others will accept our uniqueness. Take the mask off and reveal who you are meant to be. Be free from the curtain call performance. Who you are backstage is who you truly are designed to be. Be the backstage person in private, and the same person in public. No performance of impressing people is as important as being yourself. No awards, money, and accomplishments will ever have meaning if you haven't accepted yourself and accepted God. One day your curtain will close and all those people who are there to see what you can give them won't matter anymore. It will be those back stage people, who encouraged you and prepared you to pursue your purpose in the first place. The only way to get the standing ovation we long for is to fall to our knees and seek help from the One who gave us the strength to stand in the first place.

As I wrap up my final thoughts, I am going to share this poem with you. By reading this poem slowly and reflecting on the words, you will be inspired to make changes for your dash.

-DASHFULL LIFE-

When the stage of life has its lights dim
It will only matter what was within
Within your spirit, heart and mind
Only God knows when it's your time
So with the time you have been given
Give back and truly start living
Each breath in your lungs
Is a reminder that any moment you could be done
Done from the pressure of feeling lesser
No more masks and worry about your style
Just be real and smile
Be yourself because life is only a short while
As the sun sets, this could be the last time you witness God paint the sky
To all your unanswered questions we always ask why?
It's not in the why, it's what's next
 But until you reach your final destination this life is a test
Forget the mess of unnecessary stress
Don't count the problems
Count the times you have been blessed
As each day passes
 I started being who I was meant to be and stopped trying to please the masses
All those great possessions
The pursuit of them all has been depressing
Counting on people and things brings more lessons than blessings
All the mistakes, learn to look past it
It's only the photo albums that make it near your casket
The legacy left behind won't be remembered by what was mine

It will be in what I gave

I tried to change myself, but only real change came when I was saved

A promise we all have is that each day we are closer to the grave

I just want to be remembered; in 20 years will they remember my name?

Did my life matter?

Or was I obsessed with trying to climb the corporate ladder?

Where is the stairway to heaven, I heard so much about?

When I don't perform well, I begin to doubt

How could I be loved?

I tried so hard and it still wasn't enough

I know what I have seen, but I know there's something greater

Tell your loved ones you love them because you aren't guaranteed to make it to later

We are all one breath away

From which eternity we choose to call home someday

 **Author Jesse A. Cruz** lives in upstate New York with his wife and children. The Cruz family currently serves at Cross Creek Church. He has proudly served our country as an Iraq War Veteran of the U.S. Army.

Jesse is the Assistant Director of the Ontario County Youth Advocate Programs, Inc. In addition to his career, he has been engaged in speaking at correctional facilities and coaching sports. He has a B.A. in Community Youth Development at Nazareth College. Currently, Jesse is pursuing his Master's in Theology at Colgate Rochester Crozer Divinity School. In his spare time, he enjoys traveling and hiking with family and friends.

Jesse is available for speaking engagements and book signings. You may contact him directly at
authorjessecruz@gmail.com

CPSIA information can be obtained
at www.ICGtesting.com
Printed in the USA
FFHW010613170919
55040942-60731FF